Our road to adoption

DEDICATION

Our Road to Adoption is dedicated to my wife, Rebecca, and our amazing daughters. It is also dedicated to the many people who walked the road with us, and for the many who we have walked alongside.

our road to adoption

the story of our family and the great family of God

earl d robinson

First published 2018

ISBN: -10: 1717065384
ISBN-13: 978-1717065384

Contents

	Acknowledgements	Pg vii
	Preface	Pg viii
1	Chosen	Pg 1
2	The X Comes Near	Pg 11
3	September 2011	Pg 18
4	October 2011	Pg 23
5	He is Called Abraham Some Things are Worth the Wait	Pg 31
6	November – December 2011	Pg 39
7	February 2012	Pg 45
8	He is Called Moses Rescued for a Reason	Pg 51
9	March – April 2012	Pg 56
10	May – July 2012	Pg.64
11	She is Called Ruth The Moabite Redemption	Pg.72
12	September – December 2012	Pg 82
13	January 2013	Pg 87
14	She is Called Hannah The Song a Mother Could Sing	Pg 93

15 February – Early May 2013 Pg 103

16 Middle May – Summer 2013 Pg 112

17 She is Called Esther Pg 123
For Such a Time as This

18 Autumn 2013 Pg 132

19 December – January 2014 Pg 138

20 He is Called Jesus Pg 145
The Only Begotten

21 February – March 2014 Pg 154

22 April 2014 Pg 164

23 You are Called Son or Daughter Pg 174
The Great Family of God

24 May – June 2014 Pg 183

25 July 2014 Pg 191

26 You are Called Heir Pg 198
All This is Yours

27 August 2014 Pg 205

28 The Beginning Pg 216

29 An Unexpected Beginning Pg 217

ACKNOWLEDGEMENTS

There are many people to thank for the creation of this book. There are people who have encouraged me greatly, challenged me and helped me through the writing process. I have been blessed with friends who have asked how it is going and how far I've gotten. I have had established authors who thought I could do it and encouraged me that there was a book in me. I'm thankful for the willing proofreaders who have offered such helpful feedback. Very special thanks to Kate my editor who asks the right questions and makes the right changes. Another special thanks to Lannah who has shown her creative touch on the cover and promotion design.

Preface

You are about to enter a story. Many would agree it is the best way to teach. Stories are all around us; each of us have them. You might enjoy sharing them over dinner or around the campfire. They are made of memories pieced together that form some kind of drama to be shared. It might be short or long, funny or serious, a scary or tragic story. Our families are one of the likeliest sources for stories. They often date back to when we were young or special times on holiday together.

For my wife Rebecca and I, our story is one of family, not only the memories we have created, but mostly the memories of becoming family. For us, the intriguing part of our story has been the journey of the adoption process, what we experienced and how we felt about those experiences. Our story is not about how to do the process, what the best practice is and which forms to fill in, rather it is a story written in real time with the emotion you'd expect from the ups and downs of the process.

Our story is not the only one shared within these pages, there are also the stories of the great family of God, which is written about consistently throughout the Bible. These are compelling stories which often include a journey and times of waiting. I've attempted to tell the story of family and the thread of adoption by starting with Abraham and following all the way to the letters of the Apostle Paul.

Book Format

You will find the book broken down into two styles of writing. There are chapters which are retelling our adoption story in real time. Much of these chapters are based upon and include entries from my blog which was written at the time of our journey to adopting, as you will see from the dates. These blog entries are surrounded by my narrative which explains and reflects upon my words in the blog posts, and all that is conveyed within.

Alongside these chapters which mark our journey through to adoption, you will find interspersed chapters which share and open up the story and 'ideas' of family, as represented in the Bible. These contain the retelling of key events and characters, such as Moses, Ruth and Esther, to name a few.

I hope, pray and trust that you will find our story, together with the Biblical story, a more complete picture of family and how special it is to God.

Now, let me introduce you to the very beginning of our journey.

Chapter 1

Chosen

My wife, Rebecca, and I always dreamed of having children. Obviously, at first, we didn't realize that we were chosen ones who would have to travel down the winding road of adoption. We never thought we'd be involved in the process for many years. But we have been and there is a story to tell. How did we get to this point of wanting to adopt, or more accurately, how were we chosen to adopt? Let me tell you.

I invite you to think back to your elementary school years and those life-shaping moments in P.E. or gym class. Maybe you can identify with how the sides were decided in team sports. In my experience, it was usually by the teacher declaring the teams, the '1-2, 1-2 method' or by the two captains in the middle, who were fortunate enough to choose their teams. In the latter method, everyone else was sent to the wall while the captains, who were usually the only ones who knew how to play the game (or were the athletically talented duo of the group), would slowly but surely draft their teams. That's not to say the remainder of players weren't capable. There were usually a couple more who were always chosen quickly whilst the rest on the wall were still available. One by one the boys and girls would be chosen for respective teams. Sometimes kids were picked because of ability, some friendship ties and, finally, some were chosen simply because everybody had to be on a team.

In that type of P.E. class, being chosen was either an exhilarating or deflating feeling, depending on when you were selected. Thankfully, most of life does not run by the same set of rules, rather we, not some 'captain', are afforded choices to make. Daily I can choose to get up early, eat breakfast, go for a walk, go online or I can choose to lie in bed till noon. (There might be consequences for that, but it is still my choice.) We are offered choices constantly; they frame each and every minute of each day.

Within the core of adoption is this term 'chosen'. There are thousands of prospective parents who choose to embark upon the journey of adoption. Adopting is not something they are forced into, rather it is a choice. This choice is often made after careful investigation into whether this is the route for their family. There are the many pregnant women who for nine months daily face the questions and choices of what are they going to do with their baby? What about the women who have given birth but recognize that they are unable to raise their child? How about the difficult situations where the birth parents are not able to parent or don't take the parental role seriously? There are adoption agency staff, state and council-run program employees along with social workers, who all have to choose what is the best situation for a given new-born, toddler or teenager.

If Rebecca and I had a coin for each time we talked about choosing to adopt and being a couple who are chosen to adopt, we could probably buy a burger... or something even more expensive! The idea had been bouncing around our heads and hearts for eight to ten years. Like many couples, we were married fresh out of university without steady jobs. We had a mishmash of furniture, shiny new kitchen appliances and a whole bunch of dreams for our future. We had our 'wishlists' in our heads, if not written down, including traveling or living abroad, being fulfilled in our jobs, desiring to be available to what God asks of us, to raise Godly children and enjoy our life together as best friends. There are many other dreams either fulfilled or long-forgotten but embedded within that list was raising Godly children.

I had moved to Indiana where Rebecca was from and we were married at the ripe ages of 22 and 23. The dream of having and raising children was not on the front burner of our thinking initially. There was the reality of learning to live together, sharing all parts of life, somehow understanding each other's habits, all the while piecing together the money to pay for bills. At that point having little Robinsons running or crawling around was not really even on our radar. Just trying to keep our heads above water, as a young couple, was what we attempted to maintain.

One of Rebecca's goals and plans had always been to be a kindergarten teacher. After only a year of marriage, she had her own classroom and for nine years following this was her vocation. Not only was teaching a great way to make a living, it was also a type of replacement, fulfilment – being with and caring for other people's little children. We also were youth leaders in our church youth ministry and, in a way, the mothering and fathering of teens was met through the vast and various encounters with youth over the years. At one point during this youth leading, I had been working in accounting and sales for a rubber manufacturer and realized that it was not a long- term solution for me. The job came to a close and I decided that I would try my hand at substitute teaching (my mother always wished I would teach!) as a way to make some money and to see how it felt to be in the classroom.

Only a couple days into being in schools, I decided that it was a way forward for me to become a teacher. I was able to go back to university, this time for a teaching degree. This meant relying on Rebecca's wage, so we entered a period of time that would not make sense or really work to expand our family, either naturally or through adoption. After three and half years of classwork and practical opportunity, I had my own class of eager seven and eight year olds. Both Rebecca and I had so much exposure and time with children, that our internal needs of mothering and fathering were somewhat met through our jobs.

It is amazing how quickly time moves by, months into years, years into a decade and we had a stark realization – we were childless. What would that mean moving forward? We didn't have an answer for that difficult and emotive question other than knowing that adopting someday was in our plan. It wasn't so much an 'if', but rather a 'when'. It became extremely clear that our next step in life was to spend a year at King's Bible College and Training Centre in Oxford, England. We knew that this would be an intense time of learning, study and reading, as well living abroad in shared housing.

Once again, Rebecca and I were facing a time that didn't really make sense to expand our family; we were off on an intensive year abroad. Where our next stop after Bible College would be, again, we didn't know. We were quite certain that it meant adoption was out of the picture, at least for the present time. The awareness that the period of waiting was by no means over was difficult to swallow, but not impossible to live with daily. Our ten and a half months at King's Bible College were very demanding, therefore going through a pregnancy, having an infant or attempting to adopt during that year would have been taxing, if not near impossible.

Reading this you might expect that after our year abroad away from our jobs and normal lives in Indiana, that we would return there and build a family, among other things. However, there was also the possibility of living elsewhere and teaching or doing something totally different that we did not have experience in yet. While in Oxford, we inspected the idea of continuing to live there and work at King's Bible College. The opportunity never came to fruition, but our minds had wrapped themselves around the idea of permanently living in England. While we were finishing up our year abroad the question came to us 'would we be up for moving to the Basingtoke area in the South of England and helping lead a church?' After much prayer and consultation, we decided that the big move was going to be our plan.

We ended up having one calendar year back in Indiana, which was spent working hard, saving money and prepping to move. Once again, this was not a space of time when we spoke of having children or of entering an adoption process. There were simply too many unknowns as we planned on moving, selling many of our belongings and, in many respects, starting life anew.

Living in a foreign country takes much effort. Even with the common language shared between the USA and the UK, we found ourselves worn out from building numerous relationships across the church, the village where we ended up moving to and everywhere in between. One of the sacrifices in moving to the UK was again having to wait to adopt. As a result of our status of being Americans living abroad, we knew that we didn't have access to the cumbersome adoption system in the UK. This meant that once again we were thrust into the waiting room, in a way we were still on the wall waiting to be chosen.

Categorization

Whilst 'waiting', we had a lot of time to consider life and how we are seen. Let me tell you a little about my thoughts on categorization. I once listened as a Bible teacher taught about the word 'accuser' and, specifically about 'accuser of the brethren', which is found in Revelation 12:10. I'd heard teaching about that verse before, but I'd not heard the view that the Greek word for accuser means to categorize or one who 'categorizes'..., big deal, right? Think about it? How do you feel when you have been categorized into something or you are categorized as someone?

For many years, Rebecca and I were known as 'Earl and Rebecca from Goshen' or 'Youth Leaders from Goshen'. These were fine titles, as they were true. Yet they did not tell the whole story, we were also 'Earl, originally from New York, accounts payable clerk and EDI Coordinator', and 'Rebecca, originally from Oklahoma, EASE Facilitator and kindergarten teacher', to name a few jobs from our first years of marriage. But, of course, there are many of our stories which are untold when we are only known by a particular title. We can't expect people to know the whole story, rather they pick up the stories which apply to our relationship with them.

When we are put into a category or when we put others into categories, we do miss out on something of who they are. Why has this been on my mind and what does this have to do with our adoption journey, you might ask. While living in England, it seemed we were known as three things, 'Earl and Rebecca, Leaders of West Church'; 'Earl and Rebecca, "the Americans" in the village' and, eventually, 'Earl and Rebecca who are adopting'. Our 'titles' here don't fully encompass who we are, for example, most people who have only known us since moving to England, don't know that we've led ministry trips to various countries, that we started dating in Greece, or previously had a cat named Cameron... and there are numerous more crazy antics in our lives pre-England. You get used to these titles, as we have done over the last few years.

It was not our plan to be childless, but that too was one of the categories that we fitted into, whether we wanted to be in that box or not. Being in that category means that certain places are off limits, like the park, soft play, school grounds and children's parties. We always knew that this category didn't fit us, but it was where we found ourselves. Could it be that part of our calling was to be childless for a while and then break out of that category into another of 'parents'?

I have heard many speakers talk about calling and encouraging people to find their own calling, as if it is a single aspect of life that has to be mined out of the earth. "Find your calling and then you've done it, you've arrived".

What if our calling is actually a series of opportunities throughout life where we can partner with the Lord in various ways? Rather than being an entrée, it is more of a smorgasbord of various relationships, vocations, travels, hobbies etc… all for the glory of God.

The truth is for all the different parts of our lives and for all our jobs, journeys and experiences, we know part of our calling has been to adopt and like I stated before, it's been a 'when' not an 'if' question in our minds. Coming to grips with various stages where the timing wasn't right and there was not a release from God yet was not easy. Importantly, we were chosen to be a couple headed into the murky waters of adoption, but how could it possibly come about and when would we enter into the process? So many questions of how, when, where, what…it sounds a bit like the questions the twelve guys had when they were challenged by Jesus.

The Chosen Disciples

The disciples came from various backgrounds and vocations, most notably fishermen and a tax collector, but each of them had three very important facets of their lives in common. They were all called, willing to follow and each of them were suddenly living a life of faith they had not trained for. They were all called and chosen by Jesus, whether that was while they strolled by the sea, were in the marketplace or had an invitation given to them at their home. Did they expect this selection? Most likely they did not because they were busy running fishing companies, collecting taxes and working in other family businesses. Were they longing to drop all they had and follow a mostly unknown Rabbi through the back roads of Galilee, the streets of Jerusalem and beyond?

After each of them was individually chosen and accepted the challenge (these were not the guys usually picked first by the captain in P.E.!), they were thrust into a life of uncertainty and unknown. Gone were the scheduled fishing ventures, meeting with other businessmen and the comfort of the family home and community. Jesus laid it out clearly in Matthew 10:9-10

'Do not take along any gold or silver or copper in your belts, take no bag for the journey, or extra tunic, or sandals or a staff, for the worker is worth his keep.'

Later, in this same prep talk and warning session, He also says to be on your guard against men as they will hand you over to the local councils and flog you in their synagogues. The remainder of chapter 10 of Matthew is encouragement of how to handle the mistreatment that they will undoubtedly face in their journeys as disciples of Jesus. Talk about a faith walk!

What kinds of questions do you think this dozen were asking at this point? – "Is he serious?! This is the cost of being chosen? What about my family and that new fishing boat we saved up to buy? What will happen to us in that town?" Uncertainty, worry and lack of programming entered into their instantly unordered days. Gone were the simple comforts of knowing where they might lay their heads and where the evening meal was being cooked.

We had not been called away from the fishing net or to be living each day uncertain of where we will sleep that night. We had been chosen though, like all followers of Christ, to a life of discipleship and this has varied aspects for everyone. Imagine, for example, if all overseas workers were called and sent only to Southeast Asia. There would be gluttony of workers there, but what about the rest of the globe? If all disciples of Jesus were meant to lead a church fellowship, there would be the classic case of too many cooks and not enough bottlewashers.

Part of our calling has been to be childless for many years and we better understand others at this same place in life. There has also been a level of flexibility we have enjoyed that many married as long as we have don't have as an option. We have also recognized that another aspect of our 'choseness' is in having to and learning to wait.

Much like the students waiting on the wall in P.E. to be selected to team A or B, we waited to be chosen, not by God but by an expectant mother or an agency. While we had been chosen to adopt we could not move forward with raising a child of our own until being chosen ourselves. At times, it was wonderful to know that we were in a place of waiting, knowing that there is nothing more we can do, much like faith, it's all based on what He's already done.

Chapter 2

The X Comes Near

There are many atrocities throughout the world. They can range from beached whales to a lack of funding for inner city youth development or too few wells for freshwater in East Africa. This list could carry on for pages as we live on an earth that has not been fully redeemed with some 6.5 billion people who, while created in God's image, are capable of all kinds of evil. Greed, misuse of power, hate, coveting, backbiting...the list of wrongdoing carries on and leads to a seemingly never-ending roll of evils.

Everyone is affected by the problems in our world, but how much does my daily life get intruded upon by the lack of wells or funding in the inner city? Those problems (let's call them X) are not directly next to me. Those Xs are hardly on the screen of my life.

Some young ladies from our local churches felt that they should travel to Asia to witness first-hand, speak with and rescue young girls who are trapped in the ever-growing sex trafficking industry, if it can be called an 'industry'. For those English twenty-somethings, the horrific stories of girls being kidnapped and forced into prostitution is no longer an article in a magazine. It is a face, a hug, a phone call when a scared voice of a young girl is on the other end. The X has moved away from the periphery and right into the daily head and heart of these women.

When I was in university, back in the 1990s, my friend, Rob, and I decided to go on a weekend away with Habitat for Humanity. They are a charity organization that builds homes and buildings for those in need. Rob and I, along with a small team, felt good about going to this little hamlet in the mountains, to help build a new house for a disadvantaged family.

As it turns out, we didn't construct anything, rather we tore down a couple old dwellings. We had no hand in building, only in destroying. Even so, I arrived back at my dorm room quite pleased with my efforts and coming to the aid of those who needed my brawn and time. What a self-serving way to view a weekend of working with a charity. It says in John 1:14 that Jesus made his dwelling among us. In the Message, a version of the bible by Eugene Patterson, the passage is interpreted as 'Jesus moved into the neighbourhood'.

We did not move into that neighbourhood on that weekend, rather we blew in for a couple of days; didn't work all that hard; patted ourselves on the back; smirked while behind the closed doors of local residents and didn't really let their need seep in to our hearts. The X of inadequate housing in that area of the US could and should have moved closer through the experience, but it did not. On this occasion, that X stayed on the far edges. However, there are a couple of ways that the X or Xs in our lives come closer to our minds and hearts.

One of the ways, already described, is through involvement and another is when the X moves toward you. Usually, this is through circumstance, often not of your own choosing. (It came as a shock to me when my mother was diagnosed with breast cancer. The X of cancer has moved closer throughout life by knowing someone who was afflicted or a friend's family member who had the terrible disease, but it moved very quickly to the centre of my life with that highly significant diagnosis. There are millions of cancer cases per year, but when it is your mom it is no longer the 'silent killer' or the 'Big C', it becomes part of your life and story. The horrific X then moved even closer as my father-in-law was stricken with oesophageal cancer as well and passed away after a brave battle with the deadly disease. The battle has such meaning for us, the X is right there, day in and day out.

It is most likely that for you the X of cancer or some other illness has come near. We can't really avoid the difficult times and situations of life. They are not dependent upon social status or what job you have; they happen.

In his book 'Drops Like Stars', Rob Bell determines that solidarity is an art, it is a creative element in our lives. Solidarity with others causes a strengthening and heightens awareness, which we have toward a situation. For example, I am now much more aware of how others feel when their loved ones are afflicted with cancer and going through what is most often horrific treatments. I am not in that boat presently, but have been there, done that and got the t-shirt, as they say.

I fondly remember my days of going back to university to gain a degree to become an elementary teacher. Most of my classmates fell into two distinct categories. Either they were teenagers fresh out of high school that were searching for what they really wanted to do and they were eager beavers used to succeeding at whatever they put their hands to. The other groupings in most classes were people like me, who had lived some of life and were at a stage of transition. For most of us who went back to university, it was not a novel experience. We had already done the student life and this was different. There was more pressure. Many of us had spouses, some had children at home and others drove long distances all to fulfil dreams of becoming qualified teachers and to find a job in a local school. We were in the same boat, a boat where we lived in solidarity with our coursework.

During our studies, the big question was always present. Will I be able to acquire a teaching job after university studies are finished? We all talked about, thought about and worried about future teaching positions whenever we connected, especially during the final year together. Again, there was a level of solidarity between us but what is interesting is what happened as degrees were finished. One-by-one we started getting offers on teaching positions and very quickly lost contact with each other. The X of university and dreams of being a teacher that had brought us close for a couple of years was now gone; the transition had taken place. No longer were we in the same boat, rather we were scattered about all over the area into various schools and into new groups of relationships.

Two couples near to us in England have grown children and grandchildren who now live overseas as missionaries. They are embedded within local culture and customs. If you were to ask Dave or Jeremy a decade ago if the countries where their families now reside were close to their hearts, they would most likely say no. Did they spend time praying for that land, looking up news online, buying travel books and learning about their customs?

Were they eager to book flights and determine the best travel itineraries so that they could visit as soon as possible again? No, but oh how they do now. These distant lands are brought near to their hearts and minds through involvement and family who they love dearly dwelling there.

For us adoption and the plight of the unborn/unwanted child was an X that was far off in the orbit of our thinking initially. We heard of the odd situations here or there, maybe the teenager who kept her baby rather than abort, for example. Through the grapevine we'd hear of a couple who were intending to adopt. We had our own aforementioned dreams, but did not dwell on them daily. Like most Americans, we are well aware of the pro-life/pro-choice debate and the reality of abortion as a legitimate choice for so many would-be mothers. Even with all of that knowledge, adoption and the issue of the unborn was not right next to us.

Something changed in the interior of our beings when we wholeheartedly decided to take the plunge. No longer were the stories of an adopting couple simply interesting, it was becoming our story now too. The X was getting ever closer. The young mother who carried her baby to full term wasn't just a feel-good note on Facebook, it was a life given a chance, someday one of those babies would God willing be ours to love, cherish and instruct.

Reflecting back upon the verse in John 1 where Jesus moved into the neighbourhood, you find that He was not a god somewhere off in creation. He is not a God who was just waiting to cause bad things to happen or ask for impossible sacrifices. Rather He is a God who came to earth as 'my friend'. As a former youth group member of ours, Anthony, says, 'He became little and walked the lonely streets and dusty roads'. Jesus is just as aware of our situation as adoptive parents and as the cancer patient and even young girl who does not know what to do at the end of the nine-month period. He moved in and became one of us; He was hungry, thirsty and tired, much like I would be after travelling down a desert road.

To adopt has a few meanings, two of which shed more light into the theme of drawing near. One meaning is to accept and call something your own, as in the adoption of a child into a family. Another meaning is to put something into practice, as in the adoption of a new law into government.

Jesus, while fulfilling the law, also adopted humanity as His own family. He was human in every aspect, while being God as well. In addition to making humanity his own, his deity was put into practice while on the earth by healing, forgiving and ultimately being the total sacrifice for the creation He so loved and cared for. How amazing to behold that my Saviour and creator fully understand my needs and has lived with disappointment, frustration and desire. He isn't just watching from an altar built by human hands...no, He has relationship with us, He knows the desire of our hearts. There is peace and comfort which descends as you step back and realize we are not in this alone.

An X or many Xs come near in our lives for many reasons, sometimes they lead to drastic action. For us, the X of adoption was now in front of us in full view. We didn't know all that we would face as we began the journey of adoption but we did know that we were not alone.

Chapter 3

September 2011

I think that everybody enjoys an invitation, and right now I invite you into the details of our journey. Along this journey, you'll read about both my and Rebecca's thoughts, actions, concerns and you'll feel the ups and downs of the adoption process. Let's start back in the early autumn of 2011.

I wouldn't say that Rebecca and I felt under qualified to adopt as much as we felt under informed of how to go about engaging in the process. Having heard horror stories of the roadblocks, rising costs and impractical demands upon prospective parents, we were quite scared off by the possible life-changing decision. After living in England for a couple of years, catching our footing, building wide relationships and acclimatizing to a greater level of culture, we thought that it was time to open up the 'adoption chapter' of our lives.

The first place one might look is the internet and while staying up late one night a few websites came across the screen. At first, this was so exciting, until after closer inspection, we realized that our unique circumstances of being Americans living abroad was not the norm for interested couples. We could not find anything that might be a possibility for our family status. After initial frustration, we did happen across a site that looked to be a possibility and even at that our hearts leapt. A conversation, an email or two later and again the door which seemed to have been propped open ever so slightly was now closed again.

It's one thing to hold on to hope, it's another to recall and reckon with the passage in Proverbs 13:12 that says 'hope deferred makes the heart sick'. There is a second part of the verse which states that longing fulfilled is like a tree of life. For us, this verse directly applied to our great hope of adoption. It's feeling like a kid stuck indoors on a beautiful summer's day with the flu, while all the other kids in the neighbourhood are outside having a great time together. The kid hasn't done anything wrong, but he still isn't allowed to go out and play, he can only watch his friends enjoy the sunshine. For us, it was though we not only did not know where to turn or what to do; it was as though we were *not allowed to*. Unless you're at a red light, an airport without an ID or you have an empty bank account, how often are you told as an adult that you can't? As a child that's a familiar and well-worn path of frustration but as adults, married for 15 years, it's not the kind of instructions we'd expect to receive.

No matter how news is taken and circumstances are handled, life does carry on and the sun rises in the east each morning. Our days quickly turned into months and we actually 'forgot' about our plans, getting caught up in the trappings of daily living in the community with our housemates and decisions adjoined to leading the church. The months turned into over a half-year (a half-year where going into the adoption process would have been extremely difficult for a myriad of reasons) where we didn't move forward at all with our intentions. Then along came the 14th and 15th of September, days that I'll remember, just like the 27th of November is my dad's birthday or the 1st of April is the night that Rebecca and I started dating back in university, on that majestic beach in Greece; let's just say those days in September 2011 are vital to our lives.

Blog Post: 14th September 2011 - Putney Bridge and 5 Minutes

We had just arrived back at our friends' house, quite tired after the day in Southwest London at a pastor's training session. On the journey there, we were all having an interesting discussion about adoption. We were finding out more about our friends' stories as they had brought two adopted children into their family. This took place while they lived in the USA, before moving to France for a year's worth of language training, all before heading off, a couple of years ago, to the northern part of Cameroon.

That is not the normal blueprint for adoption, but what is normal? It is a winding road they had entered into many years ago. They had both praised the adoption organization they had used, along with stating how much they learned and grew in their faith through all of the twists and turns. I remember preparing in my head a battery of deeper and searching questions, when we hit heavy traffic before crossing the Putney Bridge. At that juncture we had to pay special attention to the street names and signs and discussion came to a halt. The topic of adoption never resurfaced until finishing our journey back in Oakley [where our friends live in the UK] around 8pm that evening.

There in the car we were reminded of praying together and they wanted to pray for us and our thoughts about adopting. The prayers were simple to the ear, but intensive to the heart. Those prayers and exchanges of a handful of websites lasted maybe 5 minutes but they are proving to be 5 minutes that are changing our lives.

It's one thing to have plans, it's another thing to follow through with them. We were quite determined to have a go at getting somewhere with our dreams even if we weren't sure where to start or even what the right questions were to ask...but on the 14th September it all began.

Blog Post: 15th September 2011 - The Green Couch and BT 3500

One of the prayers that ascended the previous night was to the essence of the idea that we'd be able to sit down and actually do some researching online without interruption. This may seem like a small thing but to have space where there are no other distractions is not the most common occurrence. The timing never felt right while living in Indiana and then we found ourselves moving to Hampshire and living in the south of England. The door was now closed on this particular dream of ours, or so we thought. In an attempt to keep our heads above water in a new culture, home, church, side of the road, etc… we never felt the urge to look into adoption while being in Overton [where we lived in the UK] for the first 2 ½ years. Around February 2011, we did a bit of looking online and found an agency that dealt with international adoption. But basically, each time we attempted to find out info, email, pray or talk about it, distraction, argument and frustration ensued. We didn't sense this as a 'no' rather as a 'not yet'.

Fast forward to today and the facts are that we actually researched, had an email inquiry which was answered within that day, and made a couple of phone calls. We discovered that the couple of hours on the green couch were actually quite relaxed. This was an answer to the previous night's prayer, seemingly insignificant but in actuality the jumpstart and confirmation we needed to press forward with this potential amazing journey.

The other key factor of why the 14th and 15th is so important was a phone call that I had with the embassy in London. We were attempting to find out about us using an American agency and how that could possibly work, since we presently live in the UK. The answer made our heart jump as the other end of the line confirmed that we could in fact use the American system and not have to go through the UK system.

While many of the national systems in this country are effective, the adoption process is extremely tight and the number of adoptions has plummeted over the last few years. The door is certainly closed to non-UK citizens residing here, so to hear that we could circumvent this system and legally use the American one, we were to say the least elated. That phone call while sitting on the green couch was another piece of good news and further confirmation to us.

It was on that old green couch that we decided upon using an American adoption agency. After some attempts at getting the process started, we were finally off and running. In the beginning there was much preparation, asking questions and finding the finances to kick off the journey.

Chapter 4

October 2011

I'm sure that all parents spend a lot of time thinking of who and what their sons/daughters may become. This is so very natural; what will be passed on, how they will grow, what they will believe. Ultimately, 'what is my child's destiny?' takes the forefront. Will he or she be a world changer? Will they see their dreams come true? Will they get married? There are just so many questions of how a life will take shape.

Asking these questions of life destiny, I can imagine are about as difficult as a toddler taking first steps, saying words and forming sentences; even that first day in school, or first overnight at a friend's; being grounded; having a crush; getting a driver's license; graduation and so on, the 'firsts' continue to come year after year. These are such monumental times in a life. Fathers and mothers watch after, care for and direct a child through it all.

There are so many decisions and choices to be made, for Rebecca and me without children that has been a head game, a discussion a 'what do you think about' or 'how would you handle' kinds of conversations. In October 2011, our thinking had continued to move forward. We were on our way, at least in our heads, with this dream of adoption. We were getting closer to allow our minds to not only think theoretically about parenthood, styles of discipline, decisions of what colour to paint the bedroom, but to practically put those thoughts into action.

Blog Post: 12th October 2011 – Some News and a Goal

It is another momentous day in our adventure as today we have received the email confirmation of our pre-app and the formal application paperwork. This means that we have already gone farther than ever before and have not spent any money yet. We have put ourselves out there emotionally. So far, this week has been one full of good news within the church family and now this as well, praise to the Lord! Seeing the forms opens up the fact and thoughts that this is not easy; there is much soul searching to take place as we answer questions on paper, email and soon enough will be back in Indiana.

We have an autumn half-term coming up in two weeks and the next goal that we've set is to send off this packet with all the pertinent information about our finances, family backgrounds, thoughts on adoption, etc… This seems like a daunting task but in reality why would we approach this in fear? The goal is set and we'll have to see how we get on.

Of course, getting on with something is easier said than done. I'm sure you've been in that position, you've got what seems like an insurmountable task and probably limited time but what it takes is buckling down to get started. Once started, the realization comes that it is actually not as gargantuan as expected and the whole thing ticks over until the next project comes along. For us, that was the place we found ourselves, staring down the barrel at a target which seemed a long way off and quite small, actually still hidden among the bushes, to push the metaphor even further. Life is not lived with metaphors though, but with reality, and so we carried on.

Blog Post: 19th October 2011 – Mountain Fog and the Pearl

There are some very emotional aspects to adoption which cannot be minimized. There are also some very practical aspects to the process that cannot be minimized either. These include the paperwork, travel included and the practicalities of having a larger family, for example. Maybe the most seemingly insurmountable peak is that of finance that is needed. Let's suffice to say that adopting through an agency is not terribly cheap, in fact it is very costly. In the Bible, Jesus told of the man who spotted a pearl he desired greatly. He went and sold all to purchase it. When he had sold and purchased it, he was the proud owner of a pearl at a great price. He did pay a lot, but he was in possession of the pearl. We feel this way. The addition to our family will be very costly, but in the end, we will have another new member in our family.

The plan for this blog is not to drum up finance and fundraising ideas or events, but rather to give you a peek into the financial aspect of this adventure. We are very confident that provision will be there when needed and this will come from varied sources.

The 19th of Oct is very special on this front as today we received two bits of good news, firstly my mom and dad called back to say that if we wanted to borrow some money from the life insurance policy they took out when I was born, we can. This would be without penalty and almost without cost, because of the way that it is written out we only have to pay back 5 % of what we borrow. This was quite amazing news and my mom uttered the memorable line…

"Who knew that when we took out this policy when you were a baby that some of that money may be used for another baby…"

That was quite a special phone call with them, of course their excitement is extremely unbridled. Fast forward a couple of hours and an email came through from friends who wrote that they wanted to help us and be part of the joy as well. In the email, it stated that they were going to transfer some money to our American account! What amazing news to have friends standing with us in this way. Do you know what that feels like? To have people give you money, a true gift offering, nothing expected in return but our gratitude and news of how it's going? In one night, the mountain has started to be scaled, the summit is a long way off but it can be seen through the breaks in the clouds and fog.

Adopting through an agency is expensive. There are costs which are paid to the agency as they are the ones who do the work of matching mothers with adoptive parents and they take care of the official side of the process. There is also cost with fees for courts, lawyers and legal documentation. With us living overseas we would incur transportation costs which could be quite high with flights to and from the USA. In total all of these costs we expected to be in between $25,000-35,000.

The only alternative to an agency is a government associated body. However, they are often overwhelmed with adopters and there is little chance of adopting a baby or young child through the local authorities. Therefore, we decided the agency route was best for us, despite the costs.

Blog Post: 20th October 2011 – The Giant's Causeway

It's Thursday again and our deemed day off during the

week. Usually these days are spent going shopping, seeing a movie, out to sight see or hanging out with friends, but today we resolved to accomplish some more work on the adoption front. We'd decided to call on a number of the financial bits back in the U.S. There is much information that is required on the forms, most of which is not soul searching, although some of the questions are more easily answered than others. After applying ourselves for a while and once again not having success, we thought we'd look into some other finance possibilities we have back in the U.S. I don't know about you, but making calls, waiting on the line and asking questions about info you don't really understand is not my idea of a good time. For these couple of hours though it was not hardship, in fact it was actually quite fun.

Again, we found ourselves with a mound of good news. Another life insurance policy could be borrowed against, again without a massive payback due on what we borrow. The years put in as teachers could net us some money in an annuity program and a couple of other little amounts here and there continue to make the financial climb not as steep as it did some 24 hours earlier.

We've been told that adoption is a very faith building and bold step into the wild, and it does in fact feel like that. One of the prophetic pictures that we had while at King's Bible College was of the Giant's Causeway in Northern Ireland. This is a group of large stones under the sea that can be seen from above quite easily but cannot really be seen when on the water's surface. They are there under the water, but you can't really see them, and the word said that we were to live our lives like we were on the Giant's Causeway on one rock and then blindly stepping out to the next. We will know that the rock is there but not be able to see it, but step out in faith, it is there even if just under the surface. Hey, we have moved to England and are leading a church here, so 'stepping out' is something that we have done and I'm sure will continue to happen.

Hearing good news is always welcome, isn't it? When you flip on the television or check the headlines online, how wonderful is it to see or read positive news? Good news lifts your spirits and the perspective on situations changes quickly from possible despair and loss to overcoming and victory. This is the way we felt in late October, it seemed as though what we touched worked, what we said sounded right.

Stepping onto the Giant's Causeway, in this aspect of our life, was a bit easier. The stones seemed to be right at the surface, not as slippery and maybe a bit bigger than earlier in the journey. The 24th of October came and what looked like a 'workman-like' start to the week, turned into one of those days you might even circle on the calendar in years ahead.

Blog Post: 24th October 2011 – An Envelope and a Detour

A Monday morning and it seemed like one of those days that was not going to slow down. You know what it's like when you take two steps forward and one step back, or even worse one step forward and two steps back. We had our normal prayer meeting at the office and then another meeting starting 15 minutes later. I needed to talk to a couple of people in between, in addition to printing a couple of documents too.

Rebecca had gone into town to go swimming and get a coffee, do a bit of shopping and then I'd meet her and another friend of ours at a coffee shop at 11:30ish. By 12:00 the meeting I was in ended and I was in a rush already running a half-hour late for our time at the coffee shop and having a 1:00 ministers meeting in Oakley. (Very few days are this back to back, but such is the life on certain days.) Before dashing out the door, the administrator at the churches called me into his office and closed the door behind me, this meant a level of importance higher than simply 'how do you do'? He briskly handed me a sealed envelope, he said it was for us, not from him, he was the go-between. He also stated it was not for the church, or did it have anything to do with our work for the church, it was simply for us.

When you get a surprise package like this, the mind runs quickly and you can get overwhelmed by the generosity and potential change of your situation. I had to rush off to meet our friend knowing full well that I possessed an envelope of who knows what in my bag, but I couldn't say anything to Rebecca yet. Once we did get in the car, I revealed the envelope and decided that we'd open it there and count whatever money was contained within it. Let's just say that we were blown away, the joy we experienced, the awe of a generous and faithful God seen through this gift. It was quite a car ride, we had to detour because of road works!

To be honest, I was so flabbergasted by the contents of the envelope that I struggled to help Rebecca with directions to get back to Oakley with the detours we were encountering. A couple days later we found out that the amount given to us when translated into USD (American Dollars) was within 20 dollars of the amount needed for the home study and interviews. If this is not confirmation, what is?! At this point for us, it is full speed and dead ahead.

Good news does change the look on the field, in this case more than a bit of a confirmation that we were doing the right thing at the right time. It only struck us later that without that gift we would have continued questioning ourselves, our ability to hear God and our financial position, as it relates to the adoption. The gift didn't cover it all but when dealing with steps like this process, it's more than enough for that next step. Aah, a life of faith, life lived in the vein of Abraham, if God says move then move, if He says stay then stay. The month ended by our weekly trip into town at the end of the week.

Blog Post: 27th October 2011 - The Post Office and Indy

Today, we decided to go into Basingstoke to make a visit to the bank and then a few doors down to the Post Office. Our walk into the bank to deposit the cash from Monday was a very exhilarating action - to input the money with such purpose. Then to do go down the street to the Post Office where our formal application packet was now complete and put on the scale to be weighed and priced. This packet was going off to Indy [Indiana] to the agency offices where it will be processed. For now, we wait until the emails come indicating more green lights on the road to adoption. We trust this application does not get lost on the way to Indy like the other one!

Chapter 5

He is Called Abraham
Some Things are Worth the Wait

A Call in the Night

If you are like me, you might remember the great Sunday school song called 'Father Abraham had many sons'. It was a fun song full of actions which essentially repeated that he had many sons and that we are one of them. Those are simple words to sing and do actions to but the history behind father Abraham is not so simple. In fact, he was not Abraham, his name was Abram. He was a herdsman who lived in present day Iraq. Abram was without; he had lived without children for many years, even though he was a wealthy, and no doubt respected, man in his village. At that time, a person could have all the land, animals and possessions they could accumulate and would not be complete without a family lineage to pass it onto.

I'm sure that Abram showed patience about this problem in his everyday life. He almost surely had numerous servants and farmhands who did the needed work; he most likely had advisors and other community leaders he met with to make decisions. They lived in the city of Ur, on or near the coast of the Persian Gulf in what would be considered a metropolis. Essentially, he carried on with his daily life until a monumental evening happened. It was probably like most evenings, the day's work was complete, the flocks were safe, cattle were sleeping and the estate was quiet, with most people asleep in their dwellings. This particular night was not like any other though, on this night a conversation would happen which would change history.

In Genesis 12:1-3 it states:

'Go from your country, your people and your father's household to the land I will show you. I will make you into a great nation, and I will bless you; I will make your name great, and you will be a blessing. I will bless those who bless you, and whoever curses you I will curse; and all peoples on earth will be blessed through you.'

He was awakened by God to be given the promise of blessing, not just a small personal blessing but to be the Father of the Nations. He was at this point already 74 years old, well past what would be considered 'fathering' age and his wife, Sarai, was biologically past her mothering age and capabilities. Abram didn't lack for much, he lived in his father's house, in or near a booming city, but he did not have the son to carry his family forward.

The Journey Begins

These words are radically life-changing words. They jump off the page and must have put more than a little scare into Abram. Abram was faced with a decision to respond to this command from God. Verse 4 is possibly even more shocking than the first 3 of the chapter:

'So Abram went, as the LORD had told him, and Lot went with him. Abram was seventy-five years old when he departed from Haran'

So, that was it: 'so'. The Bible doesn't say that Abram thought deeply about it or that he consulted trusted friends or leaders, he went. It sounds simple and is very easy to write, two little letters but they hold much depth. In his mind, if God spoke it then it was accurate and his response was simple, he went. Imagine you are 74 years old (for some readers that may be accurate) and the thing you need most in life you don't have and, furthermore, you can't have. We're not talking a new Ferrari or a beachside condo, it's a child, specifically a son. In the agrarian culture of the Near East 4,000 BC, sonship was the key to unlocking the future generations. When Abram listened and left for an unknown land, he did so without an heir to carry on his estate. He left with his wife, nephew, possessions and people who were part of his wealth. He was leaving his family home, what he had known for 70+ years to travel to somewhere he had never been. This did not deter him from embarking on a 1,000-mile journey down to present day Israel. While there, God spoke to him again, this time with a different promise:

12:7 – 'To your offspring I will give this land'

It probably bears repeating, he didn't have any offspring! He was not a father and his wife Sarai was passed her childbearing years by quite a margin. He built altars both in Shechem and Bethel, two areas in the land of Canaan. During a severe famine, he then proceeded to go even further south, this time to Egypt. After settling there for a while, he trekked even further south in Egypt. While going from tent to tent, he suffered through relationship issues with Lot, his nephew, and they decided to part their ways in travel. Even the small amount of family he did have were no longer staying together, yet he had this amazing promise he had heard and followed.

Another Conversation

Just three chapters after the initial conversation, Abram has another talk with God explaining that he remained childless all the while holding onto the promises from God about being the father of a nation. Abram had planned to leave his estate to Eliezer of Damascus, who was most likely his eldest servant. Abram, in speaking to God, says clearly that he wants a child, not a servant to receive his household. God responded in verses 4-5 and it must have been a 'whoa' moment to Abram:

15:4-5 – 'And behold, the word of the LORD came to him: "This man shall not be your heir; your very own son shall be your heir." 5 And he brought him outside and said, "Look toward heaven, and number the stars, if you are able to number them." Then he said to him, "So shall your offspring be.'

Have you ever been in the desert at night? Imagine there is no artificial light to hide the stars. One of the indelible memories of a visit I had to the wilderness of Israel was the uninterrupted night sky that stretched beyond what I had seen before. This is the picture God uses to help him comprehend the blessing that is coming his way. God once again promises to him that as many stars as Abram can count in the sky so shall his offspring be.

How could this be? How can one rancher who has travelled hundreds of miles and doesn't have children of his own, a man without a home, be the father of a nation? Chapter 16 in Genesis is not Abram's greatest moment. Knowing that she is unable to conceive her husband a child, Sarai encouraged Abram to sleep with her maidservant, Hagar, as a way of perhaps building a family.

Abram pursued the idea and did have a child, called Ishmael, but this was not the promised way of God as he took the situation into his own hands. After Hagar fled because of strife, God spoke to her as well and promised her that her descendants would be too numerous to count. Did it pay for Abram to deviate from God's plan? Did he show patience?

Patience is Required

Abram had shown much patience. The Bible slips in at the end of the chapter that he was 86 years at this time, meaning it was 12 years since the promise of being a father and since he made the move from his home in Haran. The story carries on, but there are 13 more years which are not recorded. It next states that Abram was 99 years old. This is an important fact to include; Abram and Sarai had waited another 13 years since the birth of Ishmael, and now a full quarter century since leaving their homeland. They had attempted to live in extreme patience with what to show for it? At that point, not much other than a story of moving from tent to tent and a birth of a child, but through another woman.

Only a God who is father could orchestrate such a family, only a God who is father could take this nomadic couple and the eventual family who arose from them to be His very own. It is in Genesis' chapter 17, at the age of 99, when God has another conversation with Abram:

17:5 – 'No longer will you be called Abram, your name will be Abraham, for I have made you a father of many nations.'

His identity has changed. With the name comes the meaning, which in this era meant even more than it does today. God changes his name; it's a statement of the promise to Abram, now Abraham. He is no longer Abram, which means 'exalted father', but now Abraham which means 'father of multitudes'.

The humanity of Abraham really shines through later in chapter 17 as God tells him that his wife, now called Sarah, whose name means 'noblewoman', will be the mother of his son. She is now 90, while Abraham is 100...I'll say that again...Sarah is 90 and Abraham is 100. Abraham laughed at God, that is quite a response, but it shows the reality of the situation. They were well past the childbirth years. How could God bring them this far, declare promise after promise, only to see them wilt in the wilderness without a family?

Abraham wasn't the only one of the couple who laughed, later in the same chapter there are three visitors who come to their dwelling. This must have been exciting and scary at the same time as they were unknown. Abraham did not realize that they were messengers from God, this time to promise that one year from then a son will be born to Sarah.

You can imagine the scene as Sarah is inside the tent working, but more listening to the talking going on outside of the tent. They asked, 'where was Sarah?' She was now at the entrance to the tent listening and when she heard the year foretold, she too laughed. The visitor heard this and you can imagine a bit of a comedic scene as Sarah eavesdrops on the conversation and is caught listening. The visitor replies to the laughter by asking the question, 'Is anything too hard for the Lord?'

100 Years Old

Genesis 21:5 – 'Abraham was one hundred years old when his son Isaac was born to him.'

When we read the account in Genesis, the writer hardly gives notice to the fact that Abraham was 100 when Isaac was born, a full 25 years after being given the promise. Often expanse of time in the Bible is understated, this is a prime example. Rather than focus on what happened through Isaac, think for a moment what might have rattled around Abraham's head.

How did I get here? This was probably a question taken both literally and figuratively. He was hundreds of miles away from what was his city and now living in tents in an unknown land. He also must have wondered how he had arrived at being the promise holder and being the dad at 100? How would he and Sarah fit in with the other 20-somethings in their camp? Surely, he thought that his God, Yahweh, had missed the mark with Abraham being the Father to the Nations, especially after holding this initial promise for 20 plus years. Much can happen in that amount of time, including the raising of a child. It's a good amount of time, imagine being in a period of waiting for 25 years. It is sort of like an airplane being in a holding pattern. It can carry on flying and waiting, but there is a runway as a destination, it is not just about flying around in circles.

Abraham had a destination given from God, it was both an unknown land which He would show him and the promise of fatherhood. He must have been immensely relieved and then immensely in awe of God even more than before. The one-year proclamation had come to pass;

a little boy had been born to him and Sarah. There were trials they faced as they raised little Isaac, even with the covenant from God in place testing in their faith level and parenthood still took place. The old adage some things are worth the wait rings true in this story.

'Patience is part of our story too'

It may feel as though the topic of waiting and acting in patience has already been exhausted with recalling our story, but it is one of the key elements of the adoption process. In our society, we so often want everything instantly. No longer is there a need to watch the nightly news, it's all there on Facebook and Twitter in real time. Going to the bank? No, do it online! Then, there is instant coffee or instant mashed potatoes! Sure, they may have some convenience, but they are not as good as the original, even if you have to wait a while.

Having and living in patience is a common trait in Biblical characters and in the development of our character. One only has to look at the amazing story of Abraham to see patience in action, the act of waiting.

Chapter 6

November – December 2011

The excitement of being accepted into the adoption process from October quickly turned into the reality of the preparation for all of the work ahead. By work, I mean travel, meetings, paperwork, emails and 'diary shifting', to name just a bit of the 'work' involved. By no means were these tasks we disdained, certainly the most difficult aspect of November was keeping this 'little secret'! At this point only my parents, Rebecca's mom, our housemate and a couple of others knew of our plans. I attempted to capture our thoughts and feeling of the moment through various blog entries during the month.

Blog Post: 19th November 2011 - Top Secret Cat

Have you ever had a secret that you were holding on to but you so desperately wanted to tell? Or maybe you've had a surprise planned for someone, like a birthday party or romantic dinner, and you couldn't wait for the secrecy to be over. That is a bit of what the last couple of weeks have been like. For us, we've been thinking and praying about this for so long that we forget that most everyone we know does not know of our plans. Here we possess a great and potentially life-changing piece of news, but still only a handful of the many people that we know are actually aware of it. The day is nearing when we can spill the beans and let the cat out of the bag, but, alas, that day is not here yet. Meanwhile, we strategize and dream about the future and what it may hold. There will be a bursting forth soon enough but for now it's still top secret and hush-hush.

The following entry comes from the day that we were able to break the news, not exactly like an expecting couple, but not too far off either.

Blog Post: 27th November 2011 - Thanksgiving and a smile

Today is the day that we get to share our news. It's not like somebody enforced this date upon us, it has been our choice. With this kind of thing, we thought it important to get far enough down the road that we actually had something to say. I suppose this could be argued, but in reality, there is still 'unsurity' about it all, until an adoption has totally gone through. This is one area where faith kicks in, if we as people could see the big picture, the details of what may be in the road ahead and know for sure how to proceed, where would the role of faith be? We can know some of what may be ahead, but not the full picture in every circumstance. With our journey, there are sure to be some setbacks and questions that we face, and in reality, the answers may not come immediately. Again, is this not where faith kicks in? In all honesty, today is not the day to be waxing theological, it is rather a day to be full-on excited.

We have an amazing church family that we have the great opportunity to lead, and today at the annual thanksgiving meeting, we were able to share our heart and where we are up to now with our journey of adoption. There were so many great stories of thanksgiving throughout the morning gathering, and many of them centered to some extent around family. So, for us to get up and come forward to share our news about extending our family was a great way to cap off the morning. It was an intense feeling to be standing there in front of those that we care so deeply for and ones who care deeply for us and mutually want the best for each other. The response that we received was what we expected, that was of happiness, more thanksgiving and many words of encouragement. A dear man in our congregation came up to me afterwards and simply said 'enjoy it, enjoy being a dad' and he had the biggest smile on his face as he gave me a hug. Rebecca was inundated with women who were excited for her.

We don't feel as though we are walking this road alone. There are many here at West Church, around Basingstoke, the UK, Indiana, Elmira and further afield who are with us as well; that too is fabulous, to have so many that care about us, how life is going for us, and what our hopes and dreams are.

As a result of using an agency in America, we knew that we'd have to take a trip to Indiana in the new year. After having sent off the paperwork, there was a lot of arranging to do for the visit. The busyness of attempting to plan the trip for the adoption training, meetings and, eventually, approval, took centre stage during these months. There were many details to sort out, including where could we stay during our month in the US; when would we meet with our adoption specialist and how often would we traverse to Indianapolis for meetings? Putting together a trip like that took much effort and planning ahead, but it proved to be only one of the big projects to put together. Following are a few clips from blogs during the December of 2011.

Blog Post: 10th December 2011 – Foot Off the Gas Pedal

You know what it's like when you've been working at

something intensely, that intensity cannot be kept up for long term. Well that is the point which we are at presently with our adoption pursuit. It may not be so much the idea of deciding to take our proverbial feet off the pedal, rather it is more the timing of it all. We are at a point where we know the next steps, i.e. what paperwork to fill in next, when to go back to America, how to proceed whilst away from our home here in the UK. Right now, we cannot really do much with any of it, outside of doing some of the form filling and admin side of things. In all reality, the pressure is off right now, it will turn up, no doubt, come February when we have many meetings, interviews, home studies etc... to take part in. But for now, we are playing a bit of the waiting game.

This may not be bad practice though, the number one question that we get asked about this process is 'when will you have a child?' and that is the one question that we cannot answer with any kind of certainty. Once again, that is a waiting position as well, we cannot control that aspect; we can control when we do certain things and how we fill-in information on forms, but not when a mother chooses us.

Interestingly though, while we are at a bit of a standstill with the process, our lives do not stop being lived. Just this week we were served notice (given our 2-month notice that we have to move), we are not shocked by this news, we knew it would come but we didn't know when. To be honest, it's not the greatest timing, but since when is there great timing for moving house?! So that leaves us in the unenviable situation of trying to find housing for two countries around the same time, can't say I saw that coming a year ago! Once again faith kicks in big-time in sticky parts of the plot like this one, we are so thankful to have a faithful God that neither leaves nor forsakes us at any point. We are at a place of peace with this newest news, even though it does throw up some new hurdles to have to be jumped in the not so distant future. Again, I suppose practice for upcoming hurdles that we cannot see yet but referring again to the Giant's Causeway we wrote about earlier in the blog (see pg 36), we step out, the rocks are there just not terribly obvious. That does not stop us from stepping out though, so off we step.

Just a few days later, after posting on Facebook that we needed a place to stay in Indiana, we received a positive response from a friend. Of course, we still had the trouble of finding permanent housing in the UK, but the following blog showed our excitement on the 21st, just a short time before Christmas

Blog Post: 21st December 2011 – Short and Sweet, should be a Tweet

I've never gotten into Twitter. I have an account but I've never tweeted or taken time to read other peoples' one-line lives, guess I'd rather actually talk to them or at least keep up via their Facebook homepage. Anyway, all that to say we have some good news concerning our trip to the States in February. A friend of ours in Goshen [in Indiana] has spoken with her parents and they have kindly offered for us to stay in their house while they are in Florida for much of the month. They also have an extra car that is parked in the garage, so we can use that too. We need to watch after the plants (this is a step of faith on their behalf), bring in the mail, and shovel the snow when it falls. We can handle that, after all this is pretty amazing news to us, having a place to stay, all of our own, was our hope but not what we expected would happen.

From there it was full steam ahead into 2012, not knowing what excitement and surprises may be around the corner of the new year. We knew we'd be living in a new house, travel to the US in February and, hopefully, have a little one to call our own. It would certainly be a year to look forward to with much anticipation.

Chapter 7

February 2012

The month that we had been waiting for was almost here: February of 2012 – a month that we felt would be life-changing for us. There had been many preparations for the month-long trip. We had made sure that the church was in capable hands while we were away and there were plenty of nervous times as we waited on a house that we thought we could move into in the UK before we left. Isn't it amazing how often trying situations come in pairs or groups? It wasn't enough we were leaving for the US for a month, we also had to move and prepare for an adoption which could happen anytime after February.

Blog Post: 5th February 2012 - Snow Melted and Bags Packed

So, it hasn't snowed even a flake all winter until yesterday. Let's just say that we were happy it wasn't tonight. Had that been the case, we would have been sweating bullets. There is a quite important flight for us to catch tomorrow morning. We are being collected at 5:30am to take the hour-long drive to Heathrow for the first traveling leg of this journey. I say traveling leg because the journey has been going now in earnest since September; it has been adventure for sure.

We've been building up to this trip to America for a while now, there are meetings on Tuesday [with the adoption agency], the day after we land, then another important one on Thursday. So, today as the temperatures rose, we were quite relieved and then we saw on the Delta website that flights were all on time and Heathrow was doing what it should, which is have planes take off and land. Tomorrow at this time, we'll be in Goshen staying the night at our home away from home. It's not only an ocean away it feels like a whole world away.

During this process we did not expect to move house, but that has also been part of this equation. We were told that we had to move out of our amazing 500-year old house right in the centre of the village because the house is going to be sold. That is fair enough, as we knew the day would come, the timing though has presented some challenges as you might expect. We have looked at one house throughout the last couple of months and yesterday we were able to give the estate agent our paperwork and deposit. In reality, it has been the only option in the village where we can continue to live with our housemate and have the space we need for our family to increase.

That's the amazing thing, we could not have adopted where we are living presently and this new place will be perfect for a family, with a fenced in back garden and all. As was written 'the best laid plans of mice and men oft go astray', in this case the plans of us men have gone astray but the plans that God has had for us is much better than ours.

Our bags are packed now, it only took an hour, I guess that comes from the experience of knowing what 23 kilos or 50 pounds feels like, and from knowing what we need in America. We also realize that when going to Indiana we always come back with more than we left with, so leaving space is a good idea. A concern one has with packing is what did you forget, in this case it's the double check again: do we have that form, or is the passport in that pocket of the bag as though it grew legs and hopped back into the desk drawer since looking 10 minutes earlier? I suppose that's nerves, probably quite normal for this kind of trip. There is much unknown in this journey which could lead to fear and, in all reality, probably will.

While in the US we had a very packed itinerary, including a meeting with our support worker and the leader of the agency in Indianapolis the day after landing in the country. After being there for a day, we were back to Goshen for our first 'home' meeting the following day, in a house that we had stayed in for one evening. All along the process our agency saw us as a unique couple and situation; they were right as we started out our meetings in a home study that wasn't our home. In addition to meeting face-to-face, there was paperwork and homework projects to do. There were books to read, an online education course, not to mention the aspect of living there for a month, involving shopping, cooking, cleaning etc... all in a house that we didn't know. Thankfully, we had a car to use and a place to lay our weary heads. Following is an entry called 'A Sweet Suite' from the 16th February 2012.

Blog Post: 16th February 2012 – A Sweet Suite

One of the aspects of this trip that we looked forward to was the traveling and one aspect that we did not look forward to was the traveling. As they say, you take the good and take the bad. Our second trip down to Indy was exactly a week after the first, we were more rested and probably better prepared for this particular trip. It was Valentine's Day, a great day for a meeting, hey?! Anyway, we decided to get a hotel for the evening rather than drive back in the late night; what a great decision that was. We logged into the hotel at 3:15 in the afternoon, enjoyed the exercise room, hot tub and our room, all before going back out for the meeting in the evening.

Earlier that day we had stopped in at the agency to drop off some paperwork for our file and we met the lead adoption specialist in the office. She surprisingly said 'we just got finished with a team meeting about you' that was not what we expected, then she invited us to sit down and we'd all go over some new information together. We had thought we'd just stop by to drop off some documents and instead we had a meeting on the spot which did prove helpful to us; a bit more understanding of how this whole process can work for us.

The evening meeting was about attachment, which is a very important subject when dealing with adoption. When, how and to what extent does an adopted child attach to the parents are key questions and this particular seminar focused on this subject. It was helpful to us, as we look to having a child attach to us in the future. After a good night's sleep, we also decided to enjoy the amenities of the hotel on the next day as well, so a hot complimentary breakfast was first on the docket. We once again used the exercise machines and hot tub, television and, eventually, checked out at 11:59. I'd say we got our money's worth on that occasion.

After being in the Goshen for about three weeks, we had 'finished' our process: the meetings, interviews, projects and training had all been completed. We waited for full approval, which would come from the office sometime after we returned back to the UK. For now, it was time to enjoy our last week or so in the US. As this summary entry below states, adoption is about children being accepted into a new family, given fresh starts, and I also talk about are our final thoughts from our life-changing trip.

Blog Post: 8th March 2012 - 'Little Ones'

There is an aspect of adoption that probably could get lost in the shuffle of all the paperwork, meetings, excitement, finance, travel, etc... and that is the fact that a little one is now part of the equation. It sounds elementary, I'm sure, but you know that having a new-born, infant, toddler, school age or teenager around changes pretty much everything. For us, we have had much experience in not having children around and we have also been overly blessed to have had so much interaction with kids of all ages. Whether that be Rebecca's nine years as a kindergarten teacher or my time with the 2nd, 3rd and 6th graders along with all other grades as a sub. Or maybe it was our 8 years working with teenagers from our church, traveling here there and everywhere, along with loads of teens from other churches as well. It feels as though we have had much opportunity with kids all over the place, from so many families, schools, churches, and many of our friends have had kids as well. Probably the ages we have the least experience is the very little ones, we're talking the newborn-toddlers. That has all been changing though, and, of course, it will change big time in the future.

As we reflect back on our great trip to Indiana, there are many things that stand out: the amazing Mexican food on various occasions, high school basketball, seeing so many friends, the generosity of people that we've seen in action, but maybe one of our favorite and most life-giving times have been spent with little ones. Many of our friends have children now and that has been part of our experience that we hang out with them and their children.

On this trip there seemed to be kids everywhere, and whether it was playing games, building blocks, shooting hoops, choo-choos, popsicle stands, jumping like a superhero, puzzles, and who knows what else, it was a blast. There is such vibrancy in their speech, often a bit louder than expected, sometimes taking everyone by surprise. There are the huge smiles while playing or running around. There are the often short stories of what happened to cause the latest 'ouchie'. Maybe it's a joke here or there that sometimes is funny, but always makes you laugh. Meal times, which usually are interesting for one reason or another, and very rarely to do with the actual food. As our trip winds down, we have to give a shout out to some of the little people who have made this trip so enjoyable and might we add preparatory in more ways than simply our adoption meetings and paperwork.

Chapter 8

He is Called Moses
Rescued for a Reason

Fast forward from the time of Abraham (see Chp 5), a number of generations and the now vast and growing family of God called the Hebrews lived in Egypt. The tribe of Hebrews had grown in population and Pharaoh, the leader of the Egyptians, declared that they have become too numerous for the Egyptians. Most, if not all of them, were slaves or servants, but the concern was if they continued to multiply in number, they would eventually take over the Egyptian people and, ultimately, the empire. The Bible even says that the land was filled with them, maybe a bit like a starry sky on a clear evening in the wilderness. An edict was written and forwarded across the kingdom that all boys born to the Hebrew people were to be killed by being drowned in the River Nile.

A Baby is Born

Along the reed covered banks of the Nile, a three-month-old baby who had been protected from slaughter was placed by his mother into an intricately woven basket and sent afloat. The name of the baby is not given at the beginning of his story. While his sister Miriam watched the basket float along, it was retrieved from the river waters by a slave of Pharaoh's daughter, who was there with her attendants to bathe.

Imagine the response on their faces when they saw the pitch covered basket contained a baby boy of only three months! Not what they expected after going down by the river. She immediately saw that it was a Hebrew baby, and who was there by that time? Miriam, the little boy's sister, who had followed along the banks of the river till he was rescued. She cleverly asked to go and find a Hebrew woman to nurse the little lad. The movie like quality of the story unfolds as his mother is the nurse and she even gets paid by Pharaoh's daughter.

In the Palace

Eventually, after he grew older, the Bible says in Exodus 2:10 that he became Pharaoh's daughter's son. He was the first person to be adopted in the big story of the Bible. She also named him Moses, which meant to draw out. Every time the name of Moses was said in the palace courts, school or playground, his story of rescue was recalled. Did Pharaoh's daughter have to wade through mountains of paperwork or go through a legal process to have Moses as her own? Most likely not, she simply laid claim to him and brought him into her family.

What a place of privilege for a little Hebrew boy who should not have been alive. He should not have been hidden for three months, nor sailed up the river and certainly not taken in by Pharaoh's court, especially his own daughter. This boy who through miraculous circumstance was nursed, fed and cared for by his own mother in the court of Pharaoh was given an upbringing unlike any other Hebrew boy in Egypt. How much did his adoption into the family of Pharaoh influence Moses?

We can't begin to say as the next story in the chapter is Moses fleeing Egypt to go to Midian, essentially to get as far away as he could. He was most likely taught to defend and fight, when he saw a Hebrew slave being beaten, he intervened. After accidently killing the Egyptian, he made sure nobody saw and he buried the body as quickly as possible. As little children learn, usually the hard way, 'be sure your sins will find you out' and this is what happened to Moses. He was a wanted man. As news of the killing spread, he skipped town to start afresh in Midian. It was while in Midian that he encountered a burning bush in which God called him to approach the throne and request the people of God to be released from slavery and Egypt.

Leaders Lead

Moses had been trained to lead. People who grew up on the courts of Pharaoh were given opportunity and the education that came with the status of being a palace dweller. During the training, it must have shined through clearly that he was a leader. I'm sure that not every boy who was reared in the shadow of the throne turned into a figure worth following. This little river-going lad did grow into a man who was followed by millions. His life carried such promise; he was one who was given leadership skills, experience and opportunity. He needed to be a great leader for the task he was predestined for from God.

He was truly rescued for a reason: to be the leader who rescued his own people. Talk about a plan and destiny for a life that had just begun. The people of God, promised to Abraham adopted by God as his own to be led out of slavery by one who understood what it meant to be taken in and be included in a family.

Moses was destined to be someone great, in reality every person has an incredible destiny placed upon them. The Apostle Paul, later in the Bible in the great prayer at the beginning of the letter to the Ephesians, talks about predestination. Paul cannot contain his excitement of the blessings and salvation through Christ and he uses this term 'predestined'. He recognizes that his readers may not agree, but they all have a destiny to be fulfilled. It's as though Paul is grasping for the right words and metaphors that will somehow be able to convey what he thinks about the immensity and awesomeness of Jesus. Right near the beginning of the prayer of exultation in verse 4-5 it reads:

Ephesians 1:4-5 For he chose us in him before the creation of the world to be holy and blameless in his sight. In love 5 he predestined us for adoption to sonship through Jesus Christ, in accordance with his pleasure and will.

Chosen, once again

That keyword of 'chosen' is once again in place. The fact that Abraham, Moses, you and I were chosen, not by chance on the 'team', but chosen for the team, shows the care and love of God. Not only chosen but before the creation of the world, before we were ever thought of by parents on this earth.

Another word that could explain the idea Paul is aiming at is 'election'. Election by God is a divine revelation, He is revealing what He desires. When you vote in an election you are revealing the candidate that you feel is the best person for the job. Paul is revealing that God desires you, and this election it says in the text is to be holy. It's not an excuse to sin and live wildly because you are holy, rather it is a call to live a holy and devoted life to the Father. Following on from this introduction, Paul moves deeper into his conviction by saying we are predestined, but for what?

The short answer is 'adoption to sonship'. This brief statement is rife with massive, life-changing ramifications. Any adoption changes lives; those of the ones being brought into a new family and those who are accepting the new members of the family. In this verse, the change is to be brought into sonship. This equates to being part of the great family of God. This is the kind of change that happened to Moses. He went from being a three- month-old in hiding to one who was reared by Pharaoh's daughter. He was in a position of being part of a new family; he didn't choose it, but he was chosen by God for this role. He was saved from the waters and selected to live in the courts of Pharaoh. His rescue led to the rescue of a whole nation, and they were destined to be the free people of God.

Chapter 9

March – April 2012

There was such excitement attached to the adoption process trip to Indiana that carried on throughout the whole of the month of February. We expected to accomplish all that we did in that space of time and it went quickly, yet we did feel away from our home in England for quite a while. We did have much happening upon arrival back in the UK, not the least of which, the daunting task of moving house. Before we reached the date of moving though, we had a very exciting day on the 16th of March....

Blog Post: 16th March 2012 – Approval Now What?

We have always looked at our trip to Indiana as one of adventure, listening to this part of our call, a certain amount of unknown territory and, of course, excitement. One of the areas of unknown territoriness (word?), was can we get everything done in a 3 1/2 week period of time planned in the States? If we could not get it all in during that space of time, then what? How could we finish the process of becoming approved to adopt? It's not like we can just hop on a plane and go back to Indy for one more meeting. Anyway, that question is one that hung around our heads for quite some time, especially in the run-up to the scheduled trip and whilst in the USA.

Most people take much more time to do the interviews, education meetings, paperwork and creation of the family profile. Most people are working alongside of those portions of the process, whereas we were there for that reason firstly, then meeting up with people secondly. On reflection, had we attempted to do a trip like that on our regular visit to Indiana, it would have proven all but impossible, but being there with that singular focus afforded us the possibility of completeness. So, without any further ado... **we are officially approved to adopt!!!**

We have been waiting for this official document for a fortnight or so, and it did, in fact, arrive tonight in our inbox. It did not contain any new information, but that does not diminish the importance of the letter or diminish the excitement of the finish line of this part of the process. The importance lies within the fact that without it we would not be able to adopt through our chosen agency. Without their being willing to adapt to our unique circumstances and continually work with us through our mountain of questions, we would not have been able to get to this point. So exactly what is this point, you might ask? Where do we go from here?

The short answer is we wait. We have done what we need to do, we are now in a position of waiting until we are chosen. I have been struck more than once by the reality of the choice we have made to enter this amazing process and now we are at a point where we are the ones waiting. Maybe the most common question of the last couple of months is, 'when? When will you know? When do you go back to the US? . . .when this? . . .when that??? We have plenty of answers, but not those. Being called to wait now is a great position to be in and yet a difficult spot. As a friend said, 'waiting is a dichotomy because you vacillate between fear that you are out of control and the freedom of having things out of control.' So, while we wait, would you be praying for us, that God would give us His peace as we live within His timing.

We were back in the UK and had a week or two to prepare and pack our belongings and to begin to understand our present situation of being an approved couple to take in a new-born from the US. Prepping to move is an all-encompassing task, but how excited we were that God had once again provided in our time of need. The day after we moved I logged into our already established internet connection to write....

Blog Post: 26th March 2012 – Movin' on to the Northwest Side

I don't know how many of you remember the sitcom called the Jefferson's that ran back in 1979 – 1984, but I do, at least from the re-runs that always seemed to be on the television. The theme song to that show was 'Movin on up' and in the case of that family, they moved on up to the east side to a deluxe apartment in the sky and, in our case, it is movin' on over to the northwest side, to a much more modern house in Glebe Meadow [still in the village of Overton].

We found out that we had to move out of our lovely dwelling on Winchester Street, and, at the time, we did not have any options of where to go. In the eleventh hour, the Lord provided a house for Rebecca, Lizzie [our housemate] and I to move into, and it is right here in the village. It is about an 8-minute walk to the Co-op [our local convenience store], rather than a thirty second walk, but we'll trade that for all the benefits of this house we now are moving into. To have this kind of house come available when it did was providence, as we were really desiring to stay in Overton, to continue living together and not to have to downsize too much. When there was nothing that was coming up for rental we were concerned, but fear never really kicked in, rather a peace that we would be taken care of.

So, after our trip to America, we knew that the next big thing on our agenda of life was to move house. They say it is one of the more stressful activities that one can go through. I'd say that this move has gone quite seamlessly and much of that can be down to the amazing people that we have had around us during the actual move and the run-up to it.

14 Winchester St. is a big house and to clean it meant many people giving it their all, and this is exactly what happened. A move like this underscores the value of community; I personally don't know how people who aren't surrounded by a loving community of friends can do something like this without professional or hired help. We have always seen our friends as our family and, in this case, it was a great day of working, eating and being together all around one goal of helping to get us from there to here. It goes without saying probably, but these same people who helped us this weekend are ones who will be around when we arrive back on this fair isle with a little addition to our family. When you need others' help is when you realize how much life

can't be lived on its own. I think that the old saying that it takes a village to raise a child is so true, we look really forward when we have opportunity to put that into real practice.

An aspect of our move that we did wrestle with was the fact that we were adopting but carrying on in peace about our housing situation. God was so gracious to us to provide another large house in the village. He is such an amazing provider; we have seen His hand of provision in other miraculous ways throughout our many years of marriage.

For those of you who have moved house, you'll know that once the shifting of boxes and the carrying of heavy furniture is finished the hard work starts. There are decisions of where to put the settee, what about that bookshelf would it look best here or there? Do we have enough space for the drum set? What about the slow cooker, it won't fit into the kitchen cupboard very easily? These kinds of issues are solved easily and quickly, but settling in still takes place over time...

Blog Post: 4th April 2012 – Settling In

Anytime that you move, there is such an unsettling. It doesn't matter how much you look forward to it or dread it. The whole action of boxing up what you own, going through the stuff and taking bags to the charity shops or the tip can be taxing. It takes time to figure out what to toss, what hasn't been used in a while, what is sentimental that needs special care or what is fragile which calls for some bubble wrap. Of course, after all the boxes, furniture and other stuff have been moved then it all has to be gone through and placed in the new abode. This takes not only time, but also quite a bit of headspace and emotion. The excitement of an empty space, the picture hooks on the wall, and the lamps needing a shade all provide an opportunity for creatively using our belongings to adorn the new house.

Making a house a home is a task and it is one that simply takes time. The question that you get the most once you've moved in is, 'have you settled in?' I can't say that I totally know what that means. Does that mean having boxes unpacked, having all your picture hooks occupied or plans for unused space? Does it mean that over the course of a couple of weeks an area you had never called your own is all of a sudden 'home'? That time does come, but not overnight, and we look forward to our new dwelling being a true home. It is getting there and, yes, we are settling in.

So, how much are we settling in with the adoption process? This is a question that we have wrestled with as there is a big difference between waiting with expectancy, each day looking at the email, hoping that 'the email' has come, which will drastically change our lives in a good way. Compared to waiting with expectancy, knowing that at some point that special email or call will arrive and we'll deal with those implications at that time. I feel like we are settling into the latter of the two, probably a more measured waiting, knowing that it could be a long time until our hopes are seen in the expanse of our family.

Settling into some kind of routine of life has been really helpful to us, since our return to the UK following our adoption process trip. It has allowed us to live 'normal' in a way (even though we've just moved house) and not simply eager for the next bit of good news. For us, this period of expectancy is an important one, whether that be 1 month or 14 months, or even longer, this time is truly in God's hands, we are the ones who are being asked to live it out.

When I sit down to the read the paper or check out the news online, I fully expect to acquire some information about what is going on in the world. There is always news to report, often an uprising in a far off land, or a horrible storm that has flattened a poor fishing village on a low-lying coast. Sometimes, exciting news takes the spotlight, like the opening ceremonies of the Olympics or a safe landing of a recent space exploration. How often is there no news and does that mean good news?

Blog Post: 17th April 2012 – Is no gnus good gnews?

This is a question that I have been asking myself, maybe not these exact words but the bigger idea, 'is no news good news?' As far as our adoption process has been going, there has not been much if any news in the last couple of weeks. Is that a welcomed break for us, or is that something that we should get frustrated about? There are many questions with this adventure and one of the biggest, if not *the* biggest, is around timing and frequency of information. It's not as if there has been nothing happening in our lives, we have come back to this fair land for 5 weeks now and in that space have moved out of and into a new house. That has been an undertaking and we can see that it has been the grace of God to not have a trip back to Indiana for adoption reasons during this ultra-busy time in our lives.

We have had what a small piece of good news as we've found a charity that gives adoption grants to parents who are adopting newborns from the US. Many of the grants out there only service either international or older children adoption. The other way that they kick in is by matching what the parents/church raise individually. We have decided that doing personal fundraising is not the way forward for us in this process. It would be fantastic though to receive some grant money for this purpose, so the plan is to do the paperwork on our next day off and hopefully get it all submitted in time for the April 30th deadline. There is plenty to do with it, but to be honest it doesn't rival the amount in the applications and actual adoption prep paperwork, so we should be able to handle it.

Back to the question of news and the frequency with which it arrives. In some respect, it is easier to have space and not have new possibilities swirling about because if your hopes aren't raised they cannot be dashed either. With that being said though we have really enjoyed hearing about a couple of situations that we might be suited for, and it's in those times when hopes raise very quickly. We have been given grace for this time, this time of not having much news and not having to change our lives dramatically, at this point. So, I suppose that for now, 'no gnus is good gnews', but when other news comes we'll be excited, you can be sure.

Chapter 10

May – July 2012

'No news' carried on being 'the news' for us, into the summer of 2012. After the excitement of the adoption process trip in February and the receiving of the approval letter in March, we had settled into our new house, and now the excitement had worn off. Most days we did check our email to see if anything about the adoption had come in, but one hadn't. When the phone rang, there was that possibility that it was our social worker from Indiana calling with 'the news', but she didn't.

One of the themes of the summer became sacrifice. It felt like we were giving up certain dreams in life to follow the dream of adoption. We had already moved to the UK four years previous, and with that very act had sacrificed some other plans.

Blog Post: 3rd May 2012 – The Keyword is Sacrifice

There are a number of words that come up often when helping lead a church; some of them are grace, salvation, love, the cross, sacrifice, freedom, etc., and the word that I want to hone in on for this blog entry is 'sacrifice'. It has been on my mind much lately. I've had quite a few people mention that what we are doing with adoption is a sacrifice. I like to think that the whole of our lives is a sacrifice, simply being willing to give away and lay down what we have. Sure, there are sacrifices with something like adoption: time, money, emotion, but surely that is all worth it. It is worth having on the block or laying on the altar.

So far in this journey we have had to 'sacrifice' some of our time, including a month in the US, well that was a great time not exactly something where we felt a huge loss, as you would when giving something up. There has been cost and there will be much more to come as the adoption goes through, but what better way to spend the money that we have saved and planned for over the years? Sure, we could go out and use money on an extravagant vacation, or buy a nicer car or various other purchases, but why not use our finance on something as special as life?

There have definitely been emotions sacrificed, but again it has been worth it, to share in the joys of new relationships we've built through this process, to be able tell stories of how God has set up various aspects of our trip and organizing the whole process. We have had some downs as well as ups, but that is reality, it's not all peaches and cream, as they say. So, for us, there is sacrifice, but we are more than willing and ready to offer what we have in all the various ways written about before. I'd rather look at other sacrifices that take place through the adoption process.

I cannot imagine what the feeling must be for a mother who has carried a life for up to 9 months and then after a couple of days this life is given to another family. An attachment that took around 3/4 of a year is physically severed and emotionally changed over the course of a couple of days after birth. This to me is huge sacrifice, to be willing to carry this life, go through the trials of pregnancy, the pain of birth all with the plan of then 'sacrificing' this child in the way of giving he or she to another.

What a bold statement, rather than taking the 'easy road' of abortion the mother fully gives life to the little one in the womb. We look with a steady gaze at the day when we adopt, when we hold the one given to us by both God and the brave lady who went through it all, not for her, but for another. We look to that day, but for now we wait until that lady makes contact with the agency and with us about the life that she would like to offer to us.

Another feature of the summer became the constant answering of the question 'have you heard anything?' or 'when will you hear?', with the answer being, sadly, 'no, we haven't.' There were many village-based fetes, jubilee celebrations and other parties, where we seemingly were coming across acquaintances. They, of course, meant well in asking, but the same query day after day becomes incredibly difficult to deal with.

Blog Post: 17th May 2012 – Phone Conversations and More

Rebecca's conversation between her and a delightful little 6-year-old:

Child: "So, when are you going to South Africa to get your baby? It is South Africa, right?"

Rebecca: "Close, it's America."

Child: "Ok, so when are you getting your baby?"

Rebecca: "When they call us and tell us, then we will get our baby. We are just waiting for the phone to ring."

Child: "So, when they call you, then you will have your baby?"

Rebecca: "Yes, but how old are you?"

Child: "I'm 6!"

Rebecca: "Ok, well, it might happen when you are 6 or it might happen when you are 7, we just don't know."

Child: "Ok, but I think it will happen when I am 6 because I will be 6 for a long time!"

Rebecca: "I hope it happens when you are 6 too, but I will tell you when it happens, we just have to wait for the phone to ring."

I'll bet if you think about it, you can remember times when you've been seated by the phone or had your mobile in your hand just waiting for that call. I can remember when I was going to get a phone call from an elementary school that I was hoping to work for and the expectation of the ring superseded almost everything else. I also remember back when I was 17 and excited about getting a first real job and expecting Pizza Hut to call to say whether or not I was going to be part of the team of making pizzas and pastas.

Those are decent examples but in all reality the phone was going to ring soon enough with the answers to my employment questions on the other end of the line. For us, presently, we know that there is a phone call or email out there at some point which will most likely be very life-changing but the fact is we don't know when this important call may come.

As you can imagine the question that we now face almost daily is 'do you know when you get a baby?' and, of course, answering this almost daily can be a bit of a drain. With the adoption not happening until the timing is right, we have no choice but to carry on living our daily lives. It's like this, when I get up in the morning I tend to think about eating breakfast, taking a shower, looking to see how the Rangers did in the previous night's ballgame, thinking through what I need to do before going out, and checking email to see if there are any pressing needs.

I don't immediately run to the phone, sit down next to it and wait for a call from the agency in America. If that were all there was daily, then that would drive us to craziness, but alas there is so much more in our lives than the adoption process which we have entered and have gotten well past the starting gate. There is the reality of leading the church. There are village relationships and activities. There is sharing our home with our housemate. There is our wide range of relationships in America that we value, etc... so there is more to do daily, than wait by the phone.

What a blessing that while we wait in faith we are encountering many other opportunities to see God at work in our daily lives. Since our lives are about being and not just off doing this and doing that, I think that we are able to keep this balance of waiting while going about daily living in a healthy balance.

The theme of constantly answering the same question and also waiting carried on through the unseasonably cool and rainy summer months. Again, the question of 'is no news, good news?' came into play. With it, came a bit of pressure, from myself really, to plow on with the blog, whilst struggling to find what to express to the loyal readers...

Blog Post: 3rd July 2012 – Newsroom and a Stopwatch

It has been a little while since last blogging about our adoption process and a few excuses could be made for this lack of updating on our journey. We could say because we are busy, so it has been really hard to find time to write, or that our computer has been in the shop now for 16 days, but these, while true, are not the real reason. The other night we watched a brand-new TV show called 'Newsroom' and one of the main points was delivering of the news in a bright accurate, interesting and attention-grabbing manner.

If there is a headliner like an earthquake, hostage situation or an important election, it's not difficult to deliver the attention-grabbing news. Is it feasible when there does not seem to be any news to bring? It's a bit like Seinfeld, the show about nothing that was ultimately about relationships, reality of daily life and connected with so many because it wasn't big story after big story. That is the way that our adoption process has been going, not really any news to report, rather it is the reality of everyday life whether involved in a church focused activity, cutting the hedges, making dinner, enjoying a game of Risk or playing the guitar. So, while we have this huge aspect of our lives bubbling away in the background, there is life being lived in the foreground.

While talking the other day, I said it was like adoption was on our hearts, but not on our minds. It's hard to gauge how true this actually is. Worry starts to creep in and the thoughts of 'is this for real?' and 'will we actually be chosen as parents?' invade the mind and the resting place of waiting for His timing start to be eroded with our own stopwatch. It is accurate to say that adoption is in our hearts, we long for this to happen in our lives and for friends that we know who are going through the same type of processes to see their dreams realized through adoption.

So, going back to the news metaphor, there really isn't any! Doesn't make for the most exciting blog in the world does it? We continue to wait much like we had in previous months, although now maybe more seasoned and measured in our waiting. The old saying 'good things come to those who wait' is accurate, and usually the waiting is an undisclosed amount of time.

If you are told you'll have to wait for 20 minutes until the table is ready in the restaurant, you simply put your name in and either carry on shopping or chatting, waiting for the call. If you go up to the hostess and she would say your wait would be 5 1/2 hours, there wouldn't be many who stay at that establishment, especially if there were others available. But what if that were the only option (I know not an accurate representation of much of the world around us) and there were no other ways to get a meal, perhaps a 5 1/2 hours wouldn't seem so crazy an amount of time to wait. We have been told to wait until chosen, whether that is 20 minutes or 5 1/2 hours we don't know, but we do know that having a little life in our care is worth the wait.

Much like the Newsroom, when there is breaking news, we'll be there for you, but until that point we'll carry on delivering the news of waiting and our thoughts/feelings about this amazing journey which we've embarked upon.

Chapter 11

She is Called Ruth
The Moab Redemption

What springs to mind when the word 'redemption' is said? Probably not too much, as the word isn't used in our everyday life all that often. You may 'redeem a voucher' for a purchase or you might think of the famed 'Shawshank Redemption' film, where the main character was ultimately set free from being imprisoned. It might be that the word is used when somebody receives forgiveness from something they have done. It certainly carries a positive meaning of a being set free or of being saved. The word 'redeemed' means to be bought back, to be purchased, but in an affirming way.

As time has gone on, the power of redemption or being redeemed has been a term lost to our everyday conversation. This has not always been the case. The action of redemption and needing to be redeemed has been incredibly prevalent in society. When a slave was redeemed, the irony was he or she was bought back in order to be set free. The slave was purchased to be brought into a place of freedom, even brought into a family. Redemption played a huge part throughout the stories of the Bible, including the story of Ruth.

It's another story which if played out as a film could be a blockbuster; a romantic film which would leave the audience in tears from start to finish. The story of Ruth speaks of family...no, it shouts of family, and standing by loved ones through the thick and thin. Staying close to those we love even through, and especially through, deep trial and heartache.

The Three Women

Three main characters emerge in the story of Ruth, set against a backdrop of famine in the land. They are Naomi, the mother-in-law, and two daughters-in-law, called Orpah and Ruth. Naomi along with her husband and two sons had moved from Bethlehem to Moab to be relieved from a famine. After living there for many years, her husband and both sons sadly passed away. This left three women without husbands. In the farming culture of the Near East, this was an almost unfathomable situation to live within. Naomi was a foreigner in Moab and now without any family, but for two daughters-in-law who were Moabites. What was she to do?

Ruth 1:8-9 – Then Naomi said to her two daughters-in-law, "Go back, each of you, to your mother's home. May the Lord show kindness to you, as you have shown to your dead and to me. May that Lord grant each of you will find rest in the home of another husband."

Her plan laid out clearly, she would ask them to go back to their home. She would then journey on her own to her home in Bethlehem to start life again. If this were a film, this would be edge of your seat time, would the women actually go home and leave her? At first, they both said, 'we will go back with you to your people.' This meant leaving all that they knew to start again.

It's hard to imagine the level of despair that was experienced with loss of life in that culture. Everything was predicated on family, on sons and daughters to carry on the family name and the family possessions. Naomi knew that not only was she without a husband and children, so too were her daughters-in-law. She could not accept they would come with her. It is when we are at a low point that God often speaks the loudest, and sometimes this is through another person.

Two Responses

After Naomi gave another passionate plea for them to change their minds and to go, Orpah did decide to return home with her family. From there she exits the story, but the heroine Ruth has an amazing response to Naomi. Her speech is the type of monologue that wins Oscars (to keep the film metaphor going!).

Ruth 1:16-18 "Don't urge me to leave you or to turn back from you. Where you go I will go, and where you stay I will stay. Your people will be my people and your God my God. [17] Where you die I will die, and there I will be buried. May the LORD deal with me, be it ever so severely, if even death separates you and me."

Can you feel the tension within her statement? At this point, Orpah has taken the offer to go back home, but

Ruth states Naomi is her family and, in a way, sees herself as Naomi's adopted daughter. Ruth was from Moab but her heartfelt response was that the Hebrew people in Bethlehem would be her people and moreover the God of the Hebrews would be her God.

Can She Do That?

In the book of Deuteronomy, as part of the law, it says that no Moabite, even to the tenth generation, shall be allowed to be part of the assembly of God. The Moabite people did not worship Yahweh. Ruth was not a worshipper of Yahweh to begin with either, but rather of the idol, Chemosh. The name Chemosh meant destroyer or to subdue, and part of the worship of this idol included child sacrifice. This idol the Moabite's worshipped was not like Yahweh, and Ruth not only decided to take on the Hebrew nation status but the worship of Yahweh too. The rules were broken, and the wall of the law which had stood for so many years had been broken down as well.

What followed was another journey, so often the stories of family found in the Bible revolve around a journey. In this case, it was from Moab back to Bethlehem. What would these two find there? I remember going back home over the years, but this was different, there was no Google Earth to see how the place looked; there were no instant news channels to keep up with the happenings in Bethlehem. It was basically 'go sight unseen' and figure it out upon arrival. They were immediately noticed on their arrival. It says that the whole town was stirred by the two women arriving.

It seems like quite a response from the townspeople, but it wasn't every day that two women travelled on their own to a new place, with no husbands or children. It must have been the talk of the town that day.

Enter Boaz

There was a man who was a relative of Naomi's, from her deceased husband's side, his name was Boaz. He was a wealthy landowner and farmer of barley. As it happens, it was barley harvesting season. Again, if it was a movie, cue the romantic music when Boaz is mentioned. It was time for Ruth to find a job, which seemed like an odd move but for a woman without any husband, but she intended to provide for her and her 'mother', Naomi.

Ruth 2:3 – 'As it turned out, she found herself working in a field belonging to Boaz'

Isn't it great how subtle the Bible can be: "as it turned out" or "it just happened" that the field was one belonging to Boaz. There aren't coincidences, just the handprints of God on people and relationships. Ruth gleans there, meaning she came behind the harvest to collect the grain that was leftover. She toils and earns favour in the sight of the foremen and in Boaz, the field owner, himself. Her story becomes known to him and all of sudden she's not nice, little Ruth, but rather loyal, determined companion and friend, as her name Ruth means.

To Glean or not Glean?

There was a law of gleaning that said there could only be one pass through the field and after that any leftover could be picked up by widows or the destitute. Boaz specifically asked his men to make sure to 'drop' sheaves so that there was a harvest for Ruth too. He was already on the lookout for her, showing care and respect for her. She has stood up for family, she has stood with family and now she is starting to be taken care of by another.

Sounds much like adopting and fostering, doesn't it? Loving dads and moms taking in children who have been part of one family being taken in by another one. There is a vast difference though; Ruth was an adult who was a grieving wife herself. The children who are in the system have either been given by choice by their birthparents, discarded by their birthparents, removed from their home or have lost their parents for another reason. They are not functioning adults who have experience of life and marriage like Ruth did. They are, however, in need of family, support, a permanent place to call home and a person or couple to redeem them into their family.

A Love Story

This is where the power of the story of Ruth and Boaz really shows itself. As Ruth and Boaz get to know each other more, Naomi finds she plays the part of matchmaker. There is another custom in place with the harvest and that is at the threshing floor. After the barley was gathered, it was taken to the threshing floor to be thrown to the wind to separate the grain from the chaff, which would be burnt. Once this work was complete, the harvester would sleep close by the pile of grain so that it was kept safe. Naomi had a clever way of getting Ruth and Boaz even closer.

Ruth 3:3-5– "'Wash, put on perfume, and get dressed in your best clothes. Then go down to the threshing floor, but don't let him know you are there until he has finished eating and drinking. [4] When he lies down, note the place where he is lying. Then go and uncover his feet and lie down. He will tell you what to do."

The scene is set for suspense as this time. She is now not only prepared to go to the threshing floor, but to secretly lie down near him and wait for him to awake. Can you imagine it? She has worked for him, spoken with him and now she is secretly lying there waiting for him to realize she's there – what a weird way to move a relationship forward. Cue the romantic music as verse nine happens, although it might not sound like much.

Ruth 3:9 – "Who are you?" he asked. "I am your servant Ruth," she said. "Spread the corner of your garment over me, since you are a kinsman-redeemer of our family."

In the culture of the day, the corner of the garment spread over another meant authority taken over that person. Ruth lets Boaz know that she is willing to be under his authority, essentially saying 'I'm willing to be married to you, if you are up for that'. She also says to him that it is because he is a kinsman redeemer of her family. Not of Naomi's family, but of hers. She totally saw herself as, and identified with, the family of Naomi.

Boaz was not only a wealthy estate owner, he was also a 'kinsmen redeemer'. This term (gaol in Hebrew) has various meanings and all of them important. A kinsman redeemer was a man who was a near relative who had responsibility and privilege to act for a relative who was in trouble, danger, a tough financial situation, been widowed or in need of vindication, for some reason. The kinsman redeemer was a savior. They came along to 'save' the near relative into a better situation. This could be redeeming property on their behalf, vindication for wrong-doing or redeeming people, literally buying them back from their situation

There's Another Redeemer

Boaz was a kinsman redeemer to Naomi, but not the closest in relation, as verse 12 says that there was a man who was closer in relation. Therefore, even if Boaz was interested, he couldn't unless the other man declined to be the redeemer. We are at a bit of an impasse in the love story. What about this other redeemer? What will he say? How will the story of Boaz and Ruth carry on?

Boaz was an upstanding man. He had fully accepted Naomi and Ruth. He had watched after them, had blessed them with extra basketfuls of grain and talked well of them both. What follows is another tense scene, this time in the village square, where the two kinsmen redeemers come eye-to-eye, not in a bad way, but in an honest conversation. Boaz asked him if he would be willing to purchase the estate of Naomi's late husband; this would secure her financial security. He said 'yes', and then Boaz dropped the next request. He would also have to take the Moabite woman into his family, if not, then he could not be the redeemer.

The Family Line to Jesus

A very important little detail about Boaz is mentioned at the very beginning of the New Testament. In Matthew 1:5, in the genealogy of Jesus, it reads that Boaz was born to Rahab, this is the same Rahab from the story of Joshua; she too was not Hebrew, rather a Canaanite who had been grafted into the family of God. Boaz understood the plight of the foreigner and those in desperate need, he'd been mothered by one. The other man declined the offer to take in Ruth. He said it might endanger his own estate. He was scared to show her care, because she was a Moabite.

This opened the door for Boaz to not only redeem Naomi's property but also redeem Ruth into his family. As they often say in fairy tales, 'they lived happily ever after'. In fact, Ruth went on to be one of only five women mentioned in the genealogy of Jesus, each of them with an interesting backstory: Tamar who was notorious for lying; Rahab, who was a known prostitute in Jericho; Bathsheba who had a relationship with King David and, finally, the virgin Mary, the mother of the Jesus. Isn't it amazing how

God consistently uses people that don't really fit into the expected category; people that are unlikely choices to be part of the story? In Ruth, we truly see a story of redemption, a purchase into a family which changed their lives and is part of the story of the ultimate redeemer, Jesus.

Chapter 12

September – December 2012

We waded into the choppy waters of adoption in the autumn of 2011, and by the time the autumn of 2012, we felt like seasoned mariners. We had the whole waiting thing down; we had completed the approval process; we had a room dedicated for a new addition and our families/friends were more than ready too. The date of the 13th September rolled around and we recognized that it was now an important date in our lives.

Blog Post: 13th September 2012 – It's Been a Year

Reflecting back on a whole year can be a tall task. It was just 365 days ago that the renewal of our thoughts and plans on adoption took place. In some respects, much has happened over the year period, but then from another angle much is still the same. Throughout the twelve months, we have, in chronological order: been on a holiday to Somerset, been informed that we'd have to move, planned our America trip, found a place to live in the village, gone to Indiana for a month, moved 2 1/2 weeks later, introduced Nooma, our lilac Burmese kitten, into our lives, had various houseguests, 3 large church/village events all affected by poor weather, enjoyed the Queen's Jubilee and Olympics here in England, been on a trip to Lithuania/Latvia and carried on with normal life and its ups and downs. (whew long sentence)! There has been plenty going on, for any of you who have moved house you know how strenuous plans can be. Acquiring the rental on a new place, transfer of funds, moving out of one house into another, coordination of the logistical side of things and what do you do with your stuff at the new one. It is much more than a two-week process.

Clearly this year has been highlighted by our adoption process and that too is a logistical, financial and administrative task which can be quite consuming. While consuming, it is also so worth it much like exercise, which is a commitment that is painful but healthy in the short and long run. Like stated before, this year has brought with it much change but also much has stayed the same as well.

Last September 13th, we were without child or children and the same applies to this 13/9 as well. This is both difficult and the norm at the same time. We are used to life without having kids to consider in all decisions, without having the extra mouth to feed, but we are more than ready for that to change. For a year now since writing this blog, our position has not changed as we carry on waiting. What will this blog entry look like on September 13th 2013 who knows? We have been around long enough to know that nothing is certain, it simply is not wise to count one's chickens before they hatch. This is not to say that all is doom and gloom, by no means! Death and taxes are all that are guaranteed, according to the saying, and in our lives, we are attempting to keep the tension between our hopes/desires and the reality of our situation at the forefront of our prayers. I do look forward to the entry on 13/9/13: what will be written, thought and what pictures will adorn the page? For now, let's simply write about 13/9/12.

Days slip into months easily, especially when life is either very hectic or when you have settled into a normal pattern of daily life. After returning from a relaxing but short holiday to Lithuania and Latvia, we hit the ground running. There was an extremely busy stretch with the church, including many extra meetings, decisions, and prayer-filled days and nights. Before we knew it, the calendar turned to November and the half-term school holiday was upon us.

Blog Post: 1st November 2012 – Life is Beautiful

These past couple of days have been interesting ones, it has been half-term so not as much going on around here. Sometimes it seems so busy with seeing people, meetings and study. All the daily activities take up space and time that it would seem almost impossible to have little ones running around. Other times, like these last two days, it would seem like the norm, like the way it should be. Not too long ago we went through the process of applying for a grant to cover some of the cost of the adoption. Finding ones that we can actually apply for and meet the criterion is a job in itself. There is much help out there for families, but most are for overseas adoption, or for special needs situations. Anyway, we did apply for one and received the news today that we were not given any help by the organization. There are simply too many applicants and not enough money. Isn't that wonderful that there are too many applications to wade through? Unfortunately, there is not enough finance for each one.

Compare that with a stat that Rebecca read the other day, which said there were 60 newborns to 1 year olds adopted in the whole of the UK in 2011. Drink that in, that's 60 adopted in a country of nearly 70 million people. Last year in the UK, 189,000+ abortions were carried out, while 60 adoptions of newborns to 1 year olds took place. Our fabulous agency in Indiana may have 10 in one month. That's one agency in one state in one month.

Within this country [UK], there are certainly many wonderful people who would love to adopt; we know some ourselves. Their stories tend to revolve around difficulty within the system and a general lack of any expediency on the part of the system. Either side of the pond, there are walls to climb over and roads to walk.

As I sit here on my couch typing, I am listening to the soundtrack to the film October Baby. If you have not heard of the movie, it is based on two real- life situations where babies who were supposed to be aborted were actually born. While the movie is not a blockbuster, has its flaws and is somewhat predictable, it does tell and show the story of the power of life. Hannah, the college freshman, who was not supposed to be has much to offer, she is very talented and carries so much possibility within her. She has been brought up without knowing her past, and when she finds out some of the truth it rocks her. She has not been raised in an open adoption, rather it has been very closed to the point where she does not really know who she is.

We are keen to engage with an open adoption, meaning one where the child is fully aware of their situation as being adopted, knowing their birth mother and father, if all parties are up for that. This might be considered an odd arrangement but how great for the child to know the one who was willing to give birth and life. We, of course, look forward to raising that child, to seeing the possibility and destiny within their life.

Some of the stats of adoption are harrowing. Little did we realize that entering into this process would open our eyes so widely to the need that exists. Could we solve the problem? No. But could we help be the solution? The famed story of the boy who slowly trod along the seashore throwing dried up starfish back into the surf comes to mind. While he was going about his business a man asked him what he was doing. He said he was saving starfish by throwing them back into the water. The man abruptly said ‘you can’t save them all’, to which the boy responded, ‘you’re right, but I’ll bet that one is pretty happy I threw him back in the ocean’. Sometimes, it is extremely simple to find reasons to give thanks, other times it can prove to be more difficult.

Chapter 13

January 2013

Confusion! You could look at that word as a way to explain the beginning of 2013. We were not sure of how long to wait on the adoption hopes in Indiana. We also didn't know about our long-term plans in the UK. Sometimes in life there are periods of not knowing which way is up and how to move forward. Very seldom in our lives have we hit a place of prolonged frustration, but this did feel like a fading away of hope that we had carried so strongly for many months.

Our homestudy was also due and lots of 'unknowns' came along with it. A homestudy is an in depth look at who you are as potential adopters. It is a series of meetings that are much like interviews. There may be questions about upbringing, parents, schooling, experience with children, along with enquiries about finances, expected parenting styles, and so much more. These meetings take place in the home, hence the name 'homestudy'. The idea is that they take place in the comfort of your own home and where the child or children will be welcomed into, once a placement happens.]

Blog Post: New Year's 2013 – Slides and Crossroads

That time of your life when hope turns to despair is not easy to live through. That turning can be instantaneous in the example of a car wreck that takes loved ones or it could be a long drawn out process of a debilitating disease. To some extent that slide downward into despair happens to everybody no matter how upbeat and positive somebody might be. In the case of Rebecca and I, we could feel our hope for the adoption starting to slide into despair. It might have been in a conversation where we hoped the 'a' word did not come up knowing that our answer of:

'No, we haven't heard anything yet'

would be received with another dejected expression accompanied by the awkwardness of what else are we going to talk about. As time carried on, the inevitable questions and comparisons to the UK system started to become less frequent and in many aspects that was much easier.

While the slide into the despair of our situation seemed to subside for quite a while in the back of our minds, we knew that March was coming and the one-year anniversary of being approved. While waiting, we knew that hope and grace were beginning to fade away. The motto of the adoption 'on our hearts but not on our minds' had also shifted as it was squarely on our minds, if not every day very close to it.

The feeling reminded me of when driving and the gas light comes on and is staying lit. I know I can still drive for a few more miles but that orange hue emanating from the dashboard reminds me every time my eye catches it that I've got to either fill up or run out and be stranded. For us, we knew that the months of waiting had taken their toll emotionally and now with the update on our homestudy being due in March, we had approached another crossroad.

Many questions abounded from: what house do we do the homestudy from (we don't live there)? How much will it cost? What other paperwork needs to be submitted? ... and a whole host of other questions. With the arrival of new questions, also comes the uncertainty of answers and what that could mean for the future. Would we need to make another trip to Indiana? If so, how difficult would that be to face family and friends in person only to say:

'we are still waiting and just here to update files.'

That myriad of copycat conversations did not sound like a very inviting situation to be dropped into. So, the slide from hope to despair concerning the adoption picked up speed in earnest after 2013 began.

This was our situation. We really felt like we needed to hear the voice of the Lord. Once again, we found ourselves resting in His caring and directing arms, from that vantage point faith is the way forward. Again, the powerful story of Abraham and Sarah came into view in our lives (see Chapter 5). Two people who left it all, moved lands, moved house numerous times, waited on promises from God and the ultimate promise of a child. We decided maybe a little venture to London would bring some respite.

Blog Post: 24th January 2013 – Field Trip to London

During a little getaway to celebrate Rebecca's birthday, I had organized a visit to the Science Museum. After taking the Central Line over to the museum district, we walked through a long pedestrian subway which led to the Science Museum, Natural History Museum and the Victoria + Albert Museum.

We saw signs for the V + A, it looked very interesting but plans are plans, so we almost begrudgingly carried on to the Science Museum.

The sounds of many children greeted us from the entrance hall, but after making our way to a short bathroom break, we were ready to go explore. Another gaggle of children was present in the main hall, a couple more school classes in the outer space hall and more in the next exhibit.

Being in a museum with many children is nothing new to either of us after years of being the adult in charge on school field trips. This was not a field trip, it was celebrating Rebecca's birthday, but everywhere we turned we were reminded of teaching, a profession we both loved. It also reminded us that we did not have a little one to be pushing around in a buggy or answering limitless questions of "why?" as one walks around a science museum.

The frustration, sadness and despair flowed out on the 4th floor corridor across from the elevators on a little solitary bench tucked right next to the wall, away from the masses. A few tears, hugs, silent prayers and the decision to go to the V + A instead was made. It was the right one for that day. The remainder of that Thursday was wonderful with honest conversation, laughs, great food and the recognition that while we were in a raw place emotionally, we were not only going to be ok but that we also felt we had a plan moving forward.

The trip to London did not bring respite rather more frustration, still recognizing that we had not been chosen by a mother from Indiana, along with the thoughts creeping in that it may never happen. What were we to do next was a huge question in our minds. In order to keep our profile being seen in the US, we had to update our homestudy paperwork.

This meant a trip back to the US. Normally, a trip to the US is welcome...more than welcome, more 'count the days down' type of waiting and with baited breath. This pending trip was not the same. I had always thought it but had never uttered that the next trip to the US would be to collect our child. The reason for the next trip was not to embrace a baby. This was lining up to be an incredibly difficult trip without good news for us or those standing with us. We did though have a bright light of good news that came at the end of the month...

Blog Post: 31st January 2013 – Homestudy?

I don't remember when we hatched the idea of our homestudy being done via Skype, but wow! did it make sense, especially for logistical reasons. Friday the 1st of Feb was when we spoke with our adoption specialist, after the usual greetings and short updates on life we floated our idea. The rest of the conversation took a turn, as most of the planned questions of meeting dates, locations, etc., would be rendered pointless if we never left Britain to update our file in Indiana.

We were told by our advisor that she needed to talk with her managers and see what the ruling would be. To not make the trip back to Indiana would save us much money and since we hadn't planned the trip we also did not have a place to stay, a car to drive or our ducks in a row from a church organizational perspective. As with other aspects of this winding road known as the adoption process, we would have to carry on waiting, this time for a response to our unique query.

Fast-forward about a week or so and I heard Rebecca race up the stairs…this either means extremely good or extremely bad news. On this occasion, her beaming radiance indicated that the news she was delivering was positive and indeed it was! The email gave clearance for the Skype call, and to our simply posting the required documents for our update, and not a difficult trip back to Goshen.

At that point, we knew that we had avoided an extremely tough trip to the US and were able to carry on with life as normal. There really is not a normal, and, for us, all was quickly going to turn abnormal. When God steps in unexpectedly, when He plots a new course and lays out the plans different from the original blueprints is when it really gets interesting. We thought that the road so far had been twisting and turning, but there was more up ahead, and greater opportunities than we could have imagined.

Chapter 14

She is Called Hannah
The Song a Mother Could Sing

There was a period of time when the nation of Israel did not have leaders. They had not had any kings or queens, like other nations around them, and the judges which had led were no longer in place. During this time, about 1150 BC, the closest person there was to a leader was the high priest. The high priest in charge of the temple was Eli. he was a man with much influence and responsibility.

Who was Hannah?

At this same time in history, there was a lady named Hannah who had an ache in her heart, she had an emptiness in her life. She desperately wanted a child, other women around her had little ones running around. Back then in Hebrew culture, it was not uncommon for men to have more than one wife, as it happened Hannah's husband Elkanah had another wife named, Peninnah, who had many children. Hannah was the first wife of Elkanah. Hannah was barren, this was a life sentence in the ancient near east.

The Bible says that Elkhanah loved Hannah, in fact, he gave her a double portion of the meat during their feasts. At this time, the highest and, arguably, the only value of a woman was her ability to give the man children. Penninah, sadly, was not a comfort to Hannah, in fact, she was the opposite as she chided her and made fun of her since she was not a mother. It's difficult to establish a comparison in today's world, it's difficult to place how high on a pedestal childbearing and childrearing was put.

Identifying with Hannah's plight

Maybe you can identify with Hannah. You have deep desires in your life, yet they feel like an impossible dream. We have been able to identify with her position, longing for children of our own. We could identify with Hannah, a deep desire that seemed out of our grasp. Thankfully, there are many ways that can help people like us, who want children, whether that be adoption, fostering or IVF.

While there are many who see their dreams realized, however, not everyone sees that child come into their life. At this point in the story, this is where we find Hannah. She is the butt of the joke and receiver of scorn from the other wife, and most likely the other women in the society.

Hannah had a different take on her situation than you might expect. Rather than be frustrated, mad or cynical, she kept a peaceful perspective. Instead of expressing her irritation outwardly, she kept silent and took her plight to the Lord in prayer. She wept and did not eat as she dealt with the situation. She had every right to be mean-spirited toward Peninnah and to be mad at God as He had not granted her greatest craving.

The Nazarite Vow

It was while the family had made their yearly pilgrimage to the temple at Shiloh where she was noticed by someone else; it was Eli, the High Priest. She was either inside the temple or sitting near the doorpost weeping, as she once again faced her situation. Verse 11 of the first chapter of Samuel is the prayer that she gave up to God while Eli was listening, it reads:

'And she made a vow, saying, "LORD Almighty, if you will only look on your servant's misery and remember me, and not forget your servant but give her a son, then I will give him to the LORD for all the days of his life, and no razor will ever be used on his head." '

What a vow to make! If and when she has a child there is a willingness to give that baby back to God, to sacrifice him for the work of the Lord. Not only for a period of time, on the mission field or to do a course, but for his life. The reference to no razor being used on his head comes from the book of Numbers, Chapter 6, and it's called the Nazarite vow. It was a proclamation of the most dedicated believers who would not allow alcohol to touch their children's lips or have their hair cut. These were examples in their lives of devotion to God. The Nazarite vow was usually for a period of time, but in her prayer, Hannah expressed this vow for the lifetime of her not conceived son.

The words she uttered in her heart that day could not possibly have been a new thought to her, but on this occasion another person, Eli, was watching her pray. Prayer is an action but with it sometimes being silent you can't always tell what is happening. While Hannah was praying silently it was clear that she was extremely devoted and fully emotionally engaged. Because her lips were moving but no sound was coming out, Eli thought that she might even be drunk. He said to put away her wine, to which she replied she had not been drinking, she had been praying.

Eli spoke, God spoke

Eli didn't question her anymore, he saw the anguish, he felt the yearning and heard the struggle coming from her heart. His next words must have hit her like an arrow as he sat at the doorpost of the temple speaking with her.

I Samuel 1:17 – "Go in peace, and may the God of Israel grant you what you have asked of him."

Did she at once believe this powerful statement from the High Priest? Did he have the influence and authority to make that kind of declaration? Could his words be that of another well-wisher saying that it will work out and be alright for her?

Trite answers and pithy statements about life's biggest struggles are not helpful. Maybe you've been on the other end of one of these comments? They sting and can be downright damaging. The old saying 'sticks and stones may break my bones but words will never hurt me' is anything but accurate. Words, even said in the friendliest, most supportive way, can still act like sticks and stones.

Telling someone who is grieving to stop worrying, crying or to 'move on' is about as unhelpful as it gets. How a person grieves a situation is totally up to them. There is no blueprint for grief. In the same way, giving false hope or saying it will all be fine to a mother who wants a child or to an adoptive family stuck in the process is hurtful and could leave lasting damage in their heart. There is not a time that a couple who are unable to conceive ever wants to be asked have they thought about having a child or even worse why are they are waiting?

I think that Eli walked along this slippery slope of conversation with Hannah, but she did not take his words as nice thoughts, she took them as life-changing. I remember back when people that we trusted shared with us pictures and objects they saw when they prayed for us. Twice in the same evening, two guys that I knew came up to me at a conference we were attending and said that they saw a catapult with the fabric part that gets pulled back being an American flag. It was right at that time we were contemplating whether or not we were to move to the UK. Just a few weeks later, another person we knew came up to us to say that he felt we would be going to a place that was well established and with castles. That doesn't sound like Indiana to me, and we knew that our next move was going to the UK. We took those words that others had heard from God, which were shared with us, in love and trust. Hannah took the words of Eli and praised God as she knew her internal cry had been heard.

Another trip to Shiloh

Admittedly, not all stories of women who struggle to conceive end up with children. It would be unfair to assume that every woman that prayed and poured out their heart was given a child. However, in the story of Hannah, her cry was heard and she did have a son. By the next year, when it was time for the yearly trip to Shiloh, she was not ready to go with the rest of the family. She asked if she could stay home until he was weaned and ready to be given to the work of the Lord at the temple. Hannah stayed home with her new son, Samuel, which means 'I have asked of the Lord'. Specifically, the name ends in 'el', which was one of the names of God in Hebrew.

By the time that Samuel had been weaned, Hannah was ready in her heart and soul to carry out the vow she had made before the Lord. She was prepared to give this only son to the work of the temple, to see him flourish in that place, under the care of Eli the priest. In fact, she said that she kept him home to prepare him to dwell in the presence of the Lord forever.

She made the trek to Shiloh to give a sacrifice to the Lord, this included three bulls, an ephah (36 pounds) of flour and a goat skin, used as a container for wine. Also, with her was her young son, Samuel, he was going to be part of her sacrifice. While she was in the temple, she encountered Eli and had another conversation with him.

This time around she asked if he remembered her. It was probably more of a nervous 'hello'. How could he possibly have forgotten her? The last time he saw Hannah she was a weeping mess, then in an instant after God spoke through Eli, she was full of hope.

How do you think Hannah reacted to this handover? Would it be with frustration that she kept her word or maybe with trepidation that Samuel would be trapped in the wrong place for the rest of his life and no longer with his adoring mother?

I Samuel 1:27-28 – '"I prayed for this child, and the LORD has granted me what I asked of him. [28] So now I give him to the LORD. For his whole life he will be given over to the LORD." And he worshiped the LORD there.'

The words of verse 27 go incredibly deep for Rebecca and me. They are words of hope which we have held tightly. We'd always hoped that if an adoption was successful that we too would want to 'give our children back to God through a dedication service and do so with joy. What Hannah did after her talk with Eli was maybe more remarkable.

Hannah's Song

Hannah sang a song. She put into words what was deep in her heart for her son, into a melody and prayer. This had been done previously in stories in the Bible, most notably by Moses after exiting from the hands of the Egyptians. Her prayer/song is moving, it is much more than just her thoughts about her son. Rather than try and break down segments of the poem, I invite you to simply enjoy reading it. Imagining that this once 'barren woman' was in the final stage of saying goodbye to her son.

I Samuel 2:1-10

'My heart rejoices in the LORD;
in the LORD my horn is lifted high.
My mouth boasts over my enemies,
for I delight in your deliverance.

2 'There is no one holy like the LORD;
there is no one besides you;
there is no Rock like our God.

3 'Do not keep talking so proudly
or let your mouth speak such arrogance,
for the LORD is a God who knows,
and by him deeds are weighed.

4 'The bows of the warriors are broken,
but those who stumbled are armed with strength.
5 Those who were full hire themselves out for food,
but those who were hungry are hungry no more.
She who was barren has borne seven children,
but she who has had many sons pines away.

6 'The LORD brings death and makes alive;
he brings down to the grave and raises up.

7 The LORD sends poverty and wealth;
he humbles and he exalts.
8 He raises the poor from the dust
and lifts the needy from the ash heap;
he seats them with princes
and makes them inherit a throne of honour.

'For the foundations of the earth are the LORD's;
on them he has set the world.
9 He will guard the feet of his faithful servants,
but the wicked will be silenced in the place of darkness.

'It is not by strength that one prevails;
10 those who oppose the LORD will be broken.
The Most High will thunder from heaven;
the LORD will judge the ends of the earth.

'He will give strength to his king
and exalt the horn of his anointed.'

Anyone who is a parent, works with children or has younger relatives wants the best for them. I asked a friend of mine who has three children what would be his advice for me. He said to help them be all that they can be; to help them discover who they are created to be. Hannah was no different. She wanted Samuel to discover who he was created to be. That turned out to the be the greatest prophet in the land. He would eventually be the man who anointed the first and second kings in the nation of Israel. He was a trusted, God fearing and wise man.

Chapter 15

February – Early May 2013

We did not expect a new plan; we were fully carrying on with the existing idea to adopt from Indiana. However, late in February, we went to the North of England for a church conference. It was one of the conferences with various speakers, all speaking broadly on the same topic. This time it was entitled 'Momentum'. Sounds innocent enough but looking back it rocked our world.

Blog Post: 21st- 24th February 2013 – ILR

One of the aspects and sometimes a highlight of leading a church is the opportunity to attend leaders' conferences from time to time. However, going away for a weekend, where we'd most likely encounter some awkward chats about how we are waiting and haven't heard anything yet, did not sound fun. At this point, at least we knew we were not headed to the US just for meetings, we were still itching to go but for the much more substantial reason of an actual adoption not more conversations about prepping to adopt.

We were excited as on this occasion we'd be staying with our dear friends, Jonny and Beth, in their new home in Middlesbrough. After the long drive, we were happy to sit back and catch up with them over a drink. Of course, we talked about our work situations, what we've been up to and our news with adoption. Later on that evening, we had another late night chat after the first meeting of the conference and I don't remember much of what was said but I do remember Beth saying:

'Indefinite leave to remain, that's important, look into it'

Some explanation is probably needed here; it's not like that statement is as famous as 'one small step for man, one giant leap for mankind', or 'I have a dream that one day...' The words about 'indefinite leave to remain' probably don't mean a great deal, if anything to you. To us those words meant a possible massive shift in our thinking and after she uttered those words my eyes locked with Rebecca almost as if saying, 'let's make sure we talk about that later.'

'Indefinite leave to remain' (ILR) is the next level of visa that we are allowed to pursue. It is only available to residents who have been continuously living in the UK for five years. (It's not citizenship, it is a level just beneath it.) We had decided that we would not/could not apply for this status. It would effectively close the door on adoption in the US and the UK too since we couldn't use the system in this country. However, little did we know that her statement would start us down the path of not only changing our minds, but radically changing our plans.

The conference was entitled 'Momentum' and one of the areas of living out faith that is gaining momentum among Christ followers is adoption. Numerous speakers shared stories of couples adopting or of a whole church fostering and adopting every child in their council. One that was striking was of a group of churches that agreed to foster or adopt every child in care in their council. That was impressive, as it meant that every child on the books was cared for under the collective wing of the church. Another guy spoke about how he and his wife have fostered and adopted, along with having natural children as well. He also stated that he was going to host a special lunch for people who would like to learn more about adoption in this country. I had a previous meeting planned but Rebecca was free and eager to attend. What would she find out? Would it be more good news and possible open-doors that we had not walked through before?

The last meeting of the conference we both found ourselves responding to the message entitled 'The Inconvenience of Obedience'. The call was for people who were willing to move anywhere in the UK for the sake of the gospel of God. Why were we responding? We both didn't understand but in unison we made the short walk to the front to join the many others who were kneeling and offering themselves to God as willing to go. We couldn't move. Our visa states specifically that I could only work for BCCs; [Basingstoke Community Churches], moving was not an option.

At no point in our lives here in the UK had we so unequivocally drawn a line in the sand that this is where we live and where God has called us to long term. The two of us going forward that morning was our statement, our expression physically of where we stood with God and ourselves. It also cemented the idea that the ILR status was our next step and something that was indeed worth looking into.

Having a shift in thinking to proceed toward the ILR status was seismic in our minds. It meant that we might need to cease our process in America without a definite possibility of adopting in the UK. It meant that once again we would find ourselves caught in between countries, again in that place of not knowing what our next step should be. This is not an unfamiliar place to be, but that does not mean that it is an easy space to dwell. What would the process look like in this country? All we knew was that it was not easy, painstakingly long and frustrating. Being American, we knew that we'd have to attain our ILR status before we could even begin again with the adoption process. That weekend was vital in our lives; it changed our thinking along with changing our hearts. We knew that we belonged/had to stay in the UK and that although not easy it could open up a UK-based adoption process too. What we didn't know was how this would affect our US application. We'd get the answer on the American side of the equation soon enough, the next day was our planned Skype call with the Indiana adoption agency.

Blog post: 25th February 2013 – The Skype Call

It had been an important weekend with the power of the conference and the rekindling of many friendships and all to be topped off with our planned Skype call on the Monday night. We were admittedly nervous not knowing exactly the way forward but we were resting in peace about our newly formed visa decision. During our call, we had a pleasant discussion, a nice catch up, some laughs and after the formal part our advisor asked if we had any other questions. Just one, a huge one... would our new visa disqualify us from using the agency and cancel our possibility of adopting? This was no lightweight question, rather one that could be the fulcrum of our on-going adoption process.

We were taken aback…no, shocked at the response given. We were told we could change our status here in the UK and they could simply shift our status there (Indiana) to be an American couple living abroad and internationally adopting from the US. Again, that is not the norm for international adoptions but as stated many times before on this blog, we're not considered the norm. It's not that abnormal for an American couple to adopt from abroad, but an American couple living abroad but actually adopting from America seems almost backward. At that moment, it was our only choice until we found out more information about the UK process. At times, figuring out adoption is a bit like being a sleuth, the clues are there, the solution is there but we've had to sniff them out over the years. The Skype conversation ended with smiles, a prayer and what looked like a clear path forward.

Maybe our situation wasn't changing much. It was amazing news and we could carry on as though nothing had really shifted. Our agency would make some changes, but we would not have to. It did feel odd to be Americans living abroad long-term, yet doing an international adoption, but from America! Not the way we had expected, but that looked to be the next steps. However, then that too changed. It wasn't an interaction with our agency advisor. It wasn't from gaining some further information. It was from Rebecca, sharing her heart in a vulnerable way, while sitting on the green couch.

Blog post: 11th April 2013 – Another Conversation on the Green Couch

Another month and a half flew by, and we had much encouraging news with the church from salvations, new people, new logo, new name and a potential new facility. All of this was bubbling away around us. Leading the church is what we do day in and day out, so to have so many encouraging stories almost caused us to fly along on auto-pilot with the adoption.

The update had been completed, our taxes had been submitted and the admin side of things was sorted (for now at least). When we come to our day off on a Thursday, we sigh deeply, and the worries/tasks of leading the church take a backseat while we relax, go shopping, out to eat and, generally, enjoy each other's company. Also, on these days is when we usually have some honest conversation about life, often mixed around games of Ticket to Ride and coffee in the red room. On this Thursday, Rebecca just came right out and said it:

'We're not going to adopt from the agency in America, I don't think it's going to happen'

I've learned to accept, trust and follow Rebecca's hunches and I agreed with her that I didn't think it would happen either. It was a bit of a surreal conversation as something that we have desired, fought for, spent money, time and unaccounted emotion on for now seemed to be out of our grasp.

It reminds me of something either dropped in water or hit into water that is just beyond your reach and slowly it drifts away or downstream. If it is a stream, then there is that possibility the object may drift back toward shore or get stopped on a rock, where it could be reached by a stick or by the hand. That's the way our process has felt, it was out of grasp again but we definitely felt that further down the metaphorical stream it would come back into reach.

The truth of the analogy is the reality of the lack of control that we have – the stream is in control. For our process, our Heavenly Father is in control and only He can orchestrate how, who, when, where and numerous other questions which we are unable to answer.

Having this type of conversation, you might expect would be deflating, depressing, the kind that takes the wind out of your sails. For us it was different, it was relief. No longer did we have to hold onto fading hope almost fooling ourselves. Rather we could get up, brush ourselves off and get back on the horse. Honesty is the best policy and for us it was very liberating to be brutally honest about what we were both thinking individually.

What if...? That is a question that we started to ask more consistently. It's a query which is cried out when fear creeps in. For us, it was creeping, actually more than creeping in, it was rushing in, as we began to worry about our future. What once seemed planned, orderly and in hand was not a secure status.

Blog post: 2nd May 2013 – Owls, Monkeys and the Isle of Wight

My birthday had come and gone, including tickets to a Rend Collective concert, three CDs, a song book and tickets to the Owl and Monkey Haven on the Isle of Wight (IOW). We had never been to the IOW but have been told by many that it is beautiful. The many are right – it is beautiful. The weather was priceless, the English Channel was a majestic blue and the whole experience of the ferry crossing was exhilarating. On the drive to Portsmouth [where we would catch the ferry to IOW], we had another one of 'those' conversations.

Only about 10 minutes from home, our talk about the adoption from America not happening surfaced again. Obviously, it was on our minds and it was not the way we expected this birthday trip to center around. Going away for our birthdays seem to bring out the deep-feelings within us. This time the question that we were verbalizing was 'what if', what if we never got a call, what if we could use the system here, what if we are too old to adopt, what if this and what if that.

It's not easy to hold so many questions in tension with the rest of life. It's almost as though our concerns and questions were buried just below the surface. If unseen, then we did not have to deal with them or see them, but, in reality, they are there. Exposing something in the light seems to make it manageable, whether it's addiction, financial trouble, or in our case uncertainty and worry. The talk proved to be another helpful time to dig deep into our thoughts and emotions, but once arriving at the port we parked our convo for the day.

Hearing the voice of God is an amazing aspect of life. We have a living Father who speaks, whether that be through the Bible, a gentle whisper or a word from a friend. We did hear from the Lord in our time of questioning, for all of your 'what ifs', there is a 'but God'. Talking about words of peace and reassurance, Rebecca blogged about this word from a friend.

Blog Post by Rebecca: 7th May 2013 – But God

When we are struggling or have questions or are confused about life, friends are amazing. They can encourage and help us have strength for whatever life is throwing our way. I am so blessed by the many friends that I have; friends here in England who have become like family, even though I have known them for only a handful of years. There are also friends who I have known nearly a lifetime back in Indiana who are so precious to me, especially as our times together are often not as long as we would like them to be. There is one friend though that is different than all of my other friends. He is my friend who sticks closer than a brother, who I can always count on, and will never, ever let me down. Jesus has seen me through thick and thin and been with me in Indiana, England, and everywhere life has taken me.

On the night of the 2nd of May, I went to bed that evening still feeling a bit unsettled. My "what ifs?" still lingered deep within my heart, even though I wanted to shut them down. I just decided I need to trust God that He would put my fears to rest but that is not always easy to do! I woke up in the middle of the night that night and, as it was still dark, thought I would look at my phone to see what time it was.

I think it was 4:00 in the morning, or something like that, but more importantly I realized that a text had come after I had gone to bed. The text was from a dear friend and it said something like this, "while I was praying for you the other I day, I felt God say, for all your 'whys and what ifs?' there is always '...but God.'"

Chapter 16

Middle May – August 2013

At this point, in May 2013, we were in no man's land. I suppose we were waiting for the voice of God to show us what was next. We understood 'But God' (see chapter 15), which was so helpful through those days of indecision. The process with the American agency had officially ceased. As difficult as it was to pull the plug on that hope, we knew it was the right decision, the one of peace. The next step was to inspect the possibilities in the UK.

Blog Post: 15th May 2013 - That's Right, I need to Call

Maybe we were scared of the answer, maybe it was procrastination, maybe it was the timing of God? I had on my list to call an adoption charity here in this country [UK]. I hadn't done it and could not seem to remember to make the call. Friends from our church, had their adoption go through at the very end of March and, of course, we were over the moon for them. While playing golf with the dad, on a beautiful spring afternoon, he mentioned to me the name of the agency that they had used. I logged the name and made a note to call.

That call wasn't made until the 15th of May. The 15th is an important day in our lives, because 3 years to the day, Rebecca's father Larry had passed away from a short battle with cancer. He was a caring man who would have been pulling for us all the way through our adoption journey.

I had contacted the council about a week previous to hear that we could, in fact, adopt in this country, but only after our new visas had totally gone through. At that point, we could inquire further with the county council. That was great news but it didn't seem like an open of a door, more one that wasn't fully latched.

The Wednesday morning of the 15th, I remembered to call [the agency], soon before having to leave to pick Rebecca up from her weekly prayer meeting with a group of ladies in the church. I didn't know it, but at that time I made the call, they were praying for us, specifically about our next step and our communication with the agency. I explained our situation briefly to the receptionist and she transferred me to the domestic department where I once again explained our situation. After I had finished, she informed that there was nothing we could do until after the visa was in our possession. Just at that point, her manager walked past and she put the phone down to talk with him.

I didn't have much faith then as I expected their chat to be fruitless to our efforts. Upon coming back on the phone, her voice was one of surprise as she exclaimed with excitement that we could in fact get started with the process right away. Before I knew it, I was giving details of our email, address, birthdates, etc... and she finished by saying that somebody from the agency would contact us in the next week to arrange an initial interview. I was gleeful and immediately phoned Rebecca to inform her of my running late, but for a very good reason this time! She was shocked and hurriedly passed on the news to the praying ladies who heard that their just offered prayer was being answered on the spot.

We've learned that waiting isn't much fun but along the way there are many cool surprises and the fact that the agency called back the next day was icing on the proverbial cake. Our thoughts about the ILR and our process were true, we were going for an interview in this country; to adopt from this country!

We couldn't believe this exciting news that we could join the process in the UK, and much sooner than we ever expected. However, this was soon tempered by the next hard knock, which came in the middle of June, on the first day of a visit from my Dad and Mom. We found the hand of God over our situation once again in the middle of the summer.

Blog Post: 17th July 2013 – Tent Dwellers - The Story of our Housing

We always felt like settlers when it came to housing, after living in the same apartment for 9+ years in Indiana. In Overton, people probably think that we are either pioneers; love the change of address or are simply unlucky in our housing situations.

Why write about our housing on an adoption blog? Rebecca and I have been told many times that we are like Abraham and Sarah, following God in faith, leaving our homeland, waiting for promises, trusting God for children and now we can add those who move from place to place and house to house onto that list. As you read on you'll hopefully recognize as we have that our Father in Heaven has miraculously been with us the whole time.

Turning up in this country almost 5 years ago we had hardly any possessions here but for some clothes, a computer, guitar and a few board games. The rental markets in the villages are incredibly quick moving and our first cottage had three on the waiting list the day it went up. After that weekend, we were first in the queue and the church here was able to secure it for us as our first dwelling.

After about a year, we felt very clearly from God the call to live in a community, to share life with others in an intimate close dwelling house-share situation. This was a step for us, but one that we were excited about taking, of course, having a place to call home that was big enough was the next step. That puzzle was solved when we were approached about renting an amazing grade 2 listed house (parts of it built before Columbus sailed the ocean blue in 1492) right in the heart of the village. In many respects, living there was a steep learning curve, and it was whilst we were there we really felt the call to walk down the adoption road. There was one major problem; this beautiful dwelling was not very suitable for little children and after an enquiry with the landlord it was decided that we could not have children and carry on living there.

After living there for a little more than two years we were told that the house was going to be sold, tough news, but after reflection we could see God's hands all over our situation. Our estate agent said, 'don't worry there's a great 4-bedroom place that is going to be available right when you need it', so in some respects kick back and relax. That mental relaxation didn't last long as a couple weeks later he shared with us that the house he had pegged for us was not going to be vacant after all, and that he did not have any other options for us either.

Then a few weeks later we ran into him on the street and he said it was going to available after all and would we like to see it that week before it went on the market. Often in life we have to wait, this was experienced in this move. Eventually, we signed on the day before Lizzie [our housemate] went on holiday and a couple of days before our adoption trip in February 2012. What peace of mind knowing that when we returned we had a new place to lay our head, and a place that was going to be long term.

We took long term to mean this was ours (we were renting but still making it ours as much as possible) we were able to transform the garden, decorate it if we like, call it home basically. When my parents came to England to visit us on the 11th of June we were gushing about how our house was going to be an impeccable place to raise children and they agreed wholeheartedly. Imagine our surprise when on return from lunch that same Tuesday there was a call from the estate agent. The tone of his voice meant this was not a 'how you doing?' chat, he was serving us notice (we had to move) within a two-month period!

We reluctantly had him over to talk in person. Lizzie, Rebecca and I all stayed downstairs while my parents sat and waited in the red room upstairs. Our fears were realized. The landlord was moving back and he intended to live in his house. On this occasion, the estate agent didn't have any leads of a place, and after surfing around the internet a bit we discovered nothing to rent either.

It's at this point when questions start to surface in the mind... what if nothing comes up? Where else could we go? Is there somewhere short term? What are our options? After a great holiday with my Dad and Mom, we turned our thoughts to 'what's next' and 'what if"? How quickly we can forget the promises of God, for every 'what if', there is a 'but God', and we hold fast to the truth of 'I will never leave you nor forsake you'.

We kicked around a few ideas, all leaving us without real answers. There was still nothing and we knew that by the 21st of August we had to move, whether we had somewhere permanent or not. So, we all carried on praying and once again there was a whole church praying for us, in fact, a prayer meeting for the men of the church was happening on the Wednesday.

We had asked many people if they knew of anything going in August, the rector (leader of the parish church in the village) was among them. The answer was always 'no'. There was nothing to rent in the village. What would we do? Rebecca and I decided to go down to the parish church and pray about this and other areas of life. After returning home, the rector called with some interesting news. He had been speaking with a lady at the school fete who mentioned in conversation they were moving and did he know of anyone who might want to rent a 3-bedroom place in the village? Remember, we had spoken with him the day before and he indicated that he knew of nothing around to rent. He quickly rang us with this news.

We attempted to hide our excitement, but after a couple of hours we had to take action and call. On the phone, we realized that we knew each other. We had taken their family a plate of chocolate chip cookies one time! Turns out they were putting the house on the rental market in two days' time. Our perusal of the house took place that night, and after walking out, the questions of housing that had rolled around our minds were being quickly answered.

Something from nothing, that's the way God works. He created from nothing, he consistently provides and, in this case, a house when there were no other suitable ones; a long term let where raising children will be a joy; smack dab in the middle of the village, walking distance to shops, parks, allotments, our church facility, friends, etc... another provision. There is a ten-day gap between moving from one house to the next and the Lord has given us space for our stuff to be stored across the street in our friend's garage. Yesterday, we also found out that we can house sit at another friend's house until it is time for us to officially move at the end of August. There are so many reasons to shout it from the mountain tops who and how God is. I don't think we are simply unlucky in our housing, for us it is our journey, one of faith, moving from here to there and finding contentment in every situation.

The summer waned on, a beautiful summer indeed with bright sunshine most days and very little rain. We were really excited for the actual adoption process to begin. We were going to be working with the agency. It was time for some training, which would take place across a number of days. For some, "training" might be a bad word or one that connotes either boredom or exhaustion but for us it was so exhilarating. After months of not doing anything practical towards adoption, we were going to be immersed in it for four days along with others who have the same hopes and dreams. Here are some of our thoughts from those days...

Blog Post: 1st August 2013 - Summer School

If you are a teacher, you'll probably agree with me that the school classroom is one of the best places to be. It's a small community of people with roughly the same focus, goals and tasks; it's informative and fun too. There is a relaxedness (word?) that takes place in that type of learning environment and that is what our four-day adoption training felt like. It was a step into the classroom, at times a primary classroom with bubbles, playdough and games, and then like a high school room with lectures and q&a, along with group discussions.

There were 20 people on the course, all brimming with excitement over the prospects of being adopters. Of course, at first, there was the quiet anticipation of 'how is this going to work'; 'are the presenters qualified or capable' and ' who is sitting across the room from me?' These are the same types of thoughts that go through anyone's mind when they begin a new course or attend a conference. All of these questions were answered very quickly, as good teachers and presenters do. The aims and format of the days were laid out, along with short intros from all speakers/attenders. The brief intros showed that there were doctors, teachers, IT guys, NHS workers, artists and many other professions present among the group.; the largest one to date for a four-day training.

We heard from many social workers, a couple of adoptive mothers, a mother who gave up a child and also the lead manager from the agency. Sometimes when you hear from the 'top dog' it is not all that informative or interesting, it's sort of like they are there because they have to, not because they want to. This short encounter was totally different!

Firstly, he gave a friendly intro to himself and then encouraged us all by stating that we were there, at that particular training, because we were invited. We would not have been sitting there if it wasn't felt that we could do the job of being adopters. He assured us that 97% of prospective adopters are approved nationally and even higher with our agency. The horror stories of the process taking years are becoming less frequently heard as the aim is to approve within 3-6 months and a child/children placed within another 3-6 months. The 3s are goals, not unhittable targets. They are the plan. The road to adopting in this country is proving to be paved and moving ahead swiftly. It's so good to be affirmed for where you are presently and encouraged for where you are headed.

One other nugget he shared with the group was that everyone had been matched with a social worker and we'd met them during the training. We had the opportunity to meet ours on Tuesday and to set the first date of many for our home-study process. We were just a bit shocked when our first meeting was planned for this Tuesday - the 6th of August! Ya! We have to move later in the month, but that is not stopping the process moving forward. We don't have our visa in hand yet but that also is not stopping it either. So, we'll sit down with her on Tuesday, and from there will map out the remainder of our meetings.

Getting into the actual process rather than just paperwork or sitting in training was really exciting. We had been through the homestudy process in America, so this was different, we already knew what to expect. Our assigned social worker was fabulous. She really took the time to understand us, to figure out who 'Earl and Rebecca' are and how we tick. Throughout the remainder of the summer, we had meetings with her a couple more times. We also moved home. It was like being in 'the land in between'.

Blog Post: 29th August 2013 - The Land In Between

Another home, another homestudy visit. Yesterday we had the great opportunity to meet with our social worker for the second time. These are really interesting meetings where we answer questions that she fires toward us. It's really not that daunting, rather quite lighthearted. Yesterday's topics covered from how we might deal with a troubled teenager to if our cat, Nooma, gets on well with little children. The meetings are about two hours long and begin with a customary cup of coffee, selection of biscuits and a catch-up. They are titled 'homestudy meetings' but essentially they are studies of us not our home, especially as we still aren't living in our home yet.

This weekend we move all of our belongings from our friend's two garages into our new house that we're renting. Our next home-study meeting will be in our actual home. We've already completed a home study in America in a house that we lodged in for three weeks and have had a meeting here in our former house and now a house where we are temporarily dwelling. We expect to be at our new house for the foreseeable future and be able to call it home. It has been both wonderful and confusing during this interim period of moving out, waiting to move in and eventually moving in. To be honest, it feels a bit like a holiday at home. It's August; we have cable TV; we're living out of suitcases, scrounging around meals and enjoying a slower pace of life, if even only for a couple of days.

The labour of moving, packing, unpacking, downsizing, running to the tip, etc... will come to an end soon and we'll be enjoying the comforts of our own house. It got me to thinking what it would be like to always be living in the interim, to be in-between as the norm. For children who are in the care system, being at a place they can't call their own is unfortunately how it usually works. Whether a child is in foster care or in a children's home facility, it is always just a place until something else happens. It is not permanent; it is in a way like living out of suitcases. Of course, for many children, they are too young to even understand what they are going through. It's the space until moving on to the next space.

I remember as a teacher having students who would arrive during the year into the classroom. Usually at first very timid then after a month or two they would begin to acclimate, build friendships and trust, only to find out that they were moving on again. A note would come into the inbox or an email stating that a certain student was no longer enrolled, and, of course, that child would go to the next school and begin the process all over again. How difficult it must be to be always in a temporary state?

For children who are awaiting adoption this is their position. While in foster care (this is a much-needed service and these homes are usually fantastic places to be), there is that possibility of having to move on to the next house, but there is also the opportunity of being brought into not only a long-term house but a family. In Psalms 68:6 it says that God puts the lonely in families – what a gorgeous picture of restoration! Although many children may have fallen through the cracks of family and society, there lies the hope that they no longer must dwell in 'the land between'. God does place the lonely, heartbroken and troubled into families.

Thankfully we are not and have not always been in that temporary state. The truth of those verses from Psalms would continue to be important to us as our homestudy process carried on and we inched closer to an actual adoption. Also, as the summer drew to a close, we were able to move into our new dwelling, one that felt perfect and where we could raise a child or children.

Chapter 17

She is Called Esther

For Such a Time as This

After many generations, the Hebrew people (the family of God through Abraham) did gain much land and became known as a powerful nation. During their history, there were very difficult periods of time and political situations they endured. From being attacked and under siege to rifling through disappointing king after king. One of the most harrowing and testing times would have been when they were attacked and again occupied as a nation, this time by the Mede/Persian Empire. Even in this occupied situation, the promises set forth from the time of Abraham and Isaac carried on throughout the journey as God's people would continue, no matter the difficult position. He never stopped being the loving father.

While struggling from the depths of being a people without a land of their own, there arose an adopted daughter. Her name was Hadassah, she would come to be known as Queen Esther. Much like Moses thousands of years before, she too was placed within the courts of the King, a Hebrew who was elevated to a prominent position in a non-God-fearing kingdom. Chapter 2 verse 7 from the book Esther gives us the full explanation of the relationship of Hadassah with her uncle Mordecai.

Esther 2:7 – 'Mordecai had a cousin named Hadassah, whom he had brought up because she had neither father nor

mother. This young woman, who was also known as Esther, had a lovely figure and was beautiful. Mordecai had taken her as his own daughter when her father and mother died'.

Hadassah

As stated above, Mordecai watched after Hadassah taking in his orphaned great-niece as his own. Much like the baby Moses being taken into the family of Pharaoh, this was probably not a legal adoption but more one of the heart; an expression of a family member seeing a child in need and being the father or mother that child doesn't have in their life.

The Mede-Persian kingdom stretched from present day India all the way to the Upper Nile region in Africa. There had been a call for girls near and far across this land to be brought to Susa (the capital) where one of the girls would be chosen as the next Queen for King Xerxes, after the previous queen, Vashti, had been removed from her position. Chapter one of the book of Esther retells this story before introducing Hadassah into the story:

There had been an extravagant week-long event with two banquets, one for the men and another for the women. The banquets were attended by leaders and their wives from many of the 127 provinces where King Xerxes reigned. During this time of revelry, much food and wine was consumed. On the seventh day the King summoned the Queen from her banquet. A simple request but one that Queen Vashti did not want to obey. There is not any explanation as to why not, but it does seem as though King Xerxes was not the easiest character to please.

Not obeying the King's command was about the worst offense one could have. It didn't matter whether it was a peasant child or the queen, he was to be listened to and immediately obeyed under all circumstances. In a fit of rage, in the middle of the banquet, King Xerxes had the Queen removed from her duties. From that moment, he was now looking for a replacement.

He doesn't sound like the kind of king a young girl would want to go before for any reason. He was going to comb the kingdom looking for the next queen. How many young girls do you think were signing up for this 'reality show'? This story, like some others in the Bible, might sound a bit like a fairy tale, but it's real. Many young girls were brought to the capital to be looked at and picked over. The expectation was that a queen would arise from the group.

Preparation

The girls were brought to Susa for a period of 12 grueling months. Each girl stayed in the harem being pampered for the fateful yet exciting day of being summoned before King Xerxes. Remember the kind of character the King was. He had his own wife relieved of her position because she wouldn't report to him, so he was rather demanding. The girls were transformed and prepared in order to be seen as perfect in the court of the king. They were also scrutinized and evaluated beyond comprehension. During this extreme preparation, the day would come when a girl would be chosen to parade before the king. Out of all the girls paraded before the king, Esther garnered his attention and approval the most. It's interesting that the Bible uses the name Hadassah at the beginning of the story, then during this portion the name changes to Esther. The meaning of Esther is star. It must be that she shone like a star to the king, as a royal crown was placed upon her head. To commemorate the occasion, a great banquet was thrown in her honour.

When Queen Esther had been chosen, she experienced the pomp and circumstance of coronation and gained an enormous amount of sudden power. At this point, she had not disclosed the fact she was Jewish (Hebrew). She was not a native Persian, rather she was a native of the people who were now the occupied subjects of the kingdom. The Jews were also the people who trusted and worshiped God, so she was not a natural fit for the role of queen in a pagan foreign land. There is precedent for God placing people into places of authority. Earlier in the Bible, Joseph, who was a Hebrew boy taken slave in Egypt, ended up being Vizier (second in command) under Pharaoh. Later, during a different exile, a teenage boy, Daniel, received much favour from a king and was given the rank of third in charge in the kingdom of Babylon.

God has a way of moving unexpected people in to positions and places that make great impact and who are then able to speak his power loud and clear. Even though Esther was an orphaned and adopted daughter, she became the Queen of the Empire.

She, along with Mordecai, decided that keeping their nationality secret would be the best option, until they were faced with crisis. Moments of crisis cause decisions to be made, as we are thrust into difficult situations, it does not always seem as though there is a right answer. For Queen Esther, finding the right answer in her crisis was not obvious either. Whilst she had a vast amount of power, learning how to wield that power was a steep learning curve.

An Unexpected Twist

An evil plot was hatched by a noble in the court, named Haman, to eliminate the Hebrews by edict of the king. In Persian law, a decree from the king was irrevocable. Haman's initial plan was directed at Esther's Uncle Mordecai because Haman hated him, but eventually the decree he encouraged the king to sign was aimed at all Jewish people. Haman so detested the people that he even offered 10,000 talents of silver to be put into the treasury for the men across the kingdom to carry out the business of enforcing this new law. This was no small plot and we've already seen what happens when the king's orders are not followed.

Esther had an attendant named Hathach who she sent as a messenger to talk with Moredecai. Hathach found him in the town square lying in sackcloth and ashes (an extreme way of showing sadness) as he mourned the eventual effect of the edict. The news of the decree with the evil plan was accurate and as Esther and her uncle talked through the messenger, Hathach, she realized she must act. In order to save her uncle and her people from being destroyed by this sinister plan, she must disclose her ethnicity. One of the messages sent through by Mordecai must have tugged at his heartstrings so greatly.

Esther 4:13-14 – 'Do not think that because you are in the king's house you alone of all the Jews will escape. [14] For if you remain silent at this time, relief and deliverance for the Jews will arise from another place, but you and your father's family will perish. And who knows but that you have come to your royal position for such a time as this?'

These are words of a loving uncle/father to a dear niece/daughter. How difficult it must have been to send that message. It's the kind that if he was texting his finger would tremble before pressing send. This note stated that she had a decision to make and it would affect her own life and all of her people too. The wisdom of Mordecai shows through at the end with the now famous line: 'such a time as this'. For all this star Esther was to do as queen, might this be the moment she shone the brightest?

She understood the role that preparation played in her own life, after being hand-picked following a year of straight preparation to meet the king. She recognized that extra preparation would be needed for another visit before the king. She sent the message through Hathach with the request for all the Jews of Susa to fast for her for three days and she'd do the same with the ladies in her court. What a tense three days this must have been. Even at the end of chapter four, Esther declares the following:

Esther 4:16b – 'I will go to the king, even though it is against the law. And if I perish I perish.'

That's a radical response!

She is a Strong Woman

A revelation of this magnitude could only come

about by approaching the king in person. There was no email or texting! This had to be face-to-face communication. Unmoved, stately, the king sat powerfully upon the throne, sceptre of authority clenched in his hands, able to order death to Esther and her people if he so desired. After drawing from within her deep, God-given well of courage, Esther did enter the court for the first time in a month and encountered the king. What would King Xerxes do? If he held out his sceptre, she could enter and have time with him; if not, there was no option. If not, Esther would be eliminated. Cue 'big sigh, exhale, walk in confidently...'

The king extended the sceptre and after probably wiping her brow she asked for a banquet with his majesty and with the noble, Haman. King Xerxes was happy for this to happen so Esther was able to buy a bit more time to summon extra courage for a request of repealing the edict of destruction upon her people. If the story so far has not had enough tension, there were more twists and turns to come.

Timing is Everything

That very night, after seeing Esther, the king could not sleep. He asked for the record of his reign to be read to him. While this was being read, a story he must not have really understood before, came to light. A while back, of all the people in the kingdom, it had been good ol' Uncle Mordecai that had exposed a threat when he had overheard a plan to kill the king. King Xerxes immediately asked what honour had been given to Mordecai. The answer was nothing; no notoriety, just a citizen doing the right thing by reporting what he had heard.

Just at that time, while the king was pondering the record of his reign, Haman came in the court, and the king had him come into the conversation. This is the same Haman who had been elevated to the second highest place in the kingdom, so when the king asked what should be done for the man who delights the king he was elated, for he thought it was him surely. It borders on comedic that Haman's answer was to robe the man and have him paraded through the city streets. He was unaware it was his adversary, Mordecai, who would be robed and honoured. Who was the man who was chosen to lead said parade through the streets of Susa? It was Haman. He was literally marching through the city streets proclaiming 'This is what is done for the man the king delights to honour'. Be careful what you wish for comes to mind.

A Revealing

Esther still had not revealed who she really was. It was at the banquet she requested where she must have been ringing her hands before speaking to the king. He asked her of her request and said that whatever it was it would be granted to her. It was time to divulge who she really was.

Esther 7:3-4 – 'If I have found favor with you, Your Majesty, and if it pleases you, grant me my life—this is my petition. And spare my people—this is my request, for I and my people have been sold to be destroyed, killed and annihilated. If we had merely been sold as male and female slaves, I would have kept quiet, because no such distress would justify disturbing the king.'

Meanwhile, Haman had also built a 75 ft. gallows outside of his house, which was specifically for Mordecai, ready for when the edict went through. After Esther's speech (see verses 3-4 above) the king asked who was responsible for the evil plot. The news broke right there in the banquet that is was Haman. He was the mastermind behind it all. Perhaps the king had not realized this before so clearly. It's not hard to imagine the explosion of anger that the king felt and showed when he found this out; the very man who had saved him from an evil plan, Mordecai, was the target of Haman's viscous plan.

Esther acted in great bravery before the king, and during yet another banquet he asked what she desired. She asked that her people be saved by a new law to overwrite the old one, stating that the Jewish people would not be harmed. This did not come easily as she fell before him weeping and pleading for the change. However, it did come and, eventually, she was actually given Haman's estate!

Many of us will face 'for such a time as this' moments in our lives. They may not be as harrowing as Esther's decision to face the king or speak up for her people but we will most likely have to take difficult decisions. Some of those difficult decisions may involve our family. Family will drive people to go to great extents and even risk their own well-being. The old saying, 'blood is thicker than water' was never more accurate than a young girl standing in the gap for her uncle (or adopted father) and her people.

Chapter 18

Autumn 2013

By all accounts, the autumn of 2013 was relatively normal in our lives. We were carrying on with our home study process, life in the church was bubbling away and we were settled into our new home. There was one potential issue that was under the surface but could become major trouble. The issue was our visas – the paperwork stating that we were indeed allowed to live in the UK. Without those official documents, not only were our adoption plans for naught, so would be our roles as church leaders, as we'd have to leave the country. Leaving the country was not in our thinking as you can expect, so getting the visas and passports was important to us. The first written foray into this potential firestorm in our thoughts was in October.

Blog Post: 3rd October 2013 – The Waiting Game

There are a few actions in life that are consistently part of the everyday; breathing, eating, walking, sleeping to name a few, may I add to our lives... waiting. I know we're not the only ones to wait. We all do. Although, it does feel like Rebecca and I get extra opportunities to perfect our waiting stances. We have actually been waiting for a phone and internet line for close to a month, so not much has been communicated lately. A communal 'ahhh', rose forth in our new house when the little light on the router turned yellow and a dial tone existed once again!

We have been expecting to attain our UK leave to remain visas. That would mean we can live here, come and go as we please (within reason) and not have to apply for visas every couple of years. There is a six- month window that the UKBA [UK Boarder Agency] promises to grant visas within, for us it has never taken long at all. So, with gusto, about 3 months ago or a bit more now, we marched into the post office and mailed off all of our documentation, including passports. The trouble is we have not heard anything yet. This is concerning on various levels, without our passports we can't travel abroad (we are planning a trip to the US in November); we don't have the assurity (word?) that this is in fact our home for the long term; we can't really move forward with adoption plans; we don't have some major forms of I.D. and, lastly, we can't even check on the status as there is no number, website or person to enquire with. It's not the worst, nobody has been seriously injured or been fired from a job with a huge mortgage to pay, but wow would we love to see that registered piece of mail arrive at our door.

The other day, I unfortunately left my bankcard at a local grocery store. I didn't realize it until a couple of days later. After a phone call, they confirmed that they did have the card and I could pick it up from them at the customer service desk. The next day, after showing them my driver's license I.D., I was informed that my card had been destroyed, since it had not been picked up within a certain time of being found. OK after getting over that I went to the bank to acquire a new card. I handed them my I.D. but the addresses didn't match. Rebecca and I happened to be passing the bank the day or so after moving and we changed our address, as you are meant to do, but we had not done it yet with the driver's license (no internet etc...) so then I had to prove that I was who I said I was. After some confusion, it was determined that they would put a new card in the post and it would arrive in a couple of days. Alas we wait, not only for our driver's licenses with updated addresses but now for a bankcard too. I forgot my wallet yesterday then remembered there isn't much in there that I can use anyhow!

We look forward with anticipation when all of the above is sorted out, but until that time the arrival of the postman brings a rush of excitement each and every day. At least now we have moved, we have settled into our new abode, we are back online, so we're not waiting for everything.

Our wait did continue and went from being in the back our minds to the forefront. The postman coming daily brought excitement only to be usually followed by frustration, as it was only a bill or a useless piece of junk mail that was delivered.

Blog Post: 24th October 2013 - Chugging along

When last a blog post was put up we were in full-on waiting mode for various documents, some more important than others. You will be relieved to hear, since that update we have gotten bankcards sorted and driver's licenses have come through the post, but what has not turned up is our visa/passport packet. This is obviously a big issue to us as it impedes our lives greatly without the documentation. This does not mean that we are worried about the status; we don't expect any trouble with being approved. We have not had communication stating that there are issues. We simply have not been on the receiving end of the documents yet.

For quite a while it was not really on our minds, there were plenty of other aspects of life on our minds, but not the visa/passport. Now, we have the whole church praying, and many others who are concerned, so we don't feel alone in this at all. The church family that we lead here in Overton has been so supportive and intensely interested in the whole process, really from the beginning up until now. They are an amazing group of people, ones that we have come to experience as family and as friends.

As we have gotten closer to the planned USA travel dates in November of this year, our excitement has risen to see many friends and our small families back in the States. We do look so forward to seeing so many familiar faces as we have always been so supported with our move here and certainly with the adoption process. It has been over two years now since we first jumped into the deep water of adoption, by nervously making phone calls and sending emails seeking to see if we would be eligible, even though living abroad. Of course, now involved in the process here in the UK, it feels as though we have come full circle, alas we are not finished with the process here either.

We have had three home-study meetings with two more planned in the next couple of weeks. These are quite laid back meetings at our house and there are some homework questions that we complete before each one. Mostly, it is either looking back at childhood or looking forward to how we would raise children. It feels as though the train keeps going on down the tracks that are laid, maybe not as quick as we would like, but it's chugging along.

Some days stick out in the mind as there are indelible memories made which are not easily erased. On your wedding day, for example, you might expect to create these special memories, or on a holiday while spending time at world famous sites. Unlike these example, the 30th

October was a regular day, we were simply home not doing much to be honest!

Blog Post: 30th October 2013 - Can you take me higher? the 30th what a day!

Our visa and indefinite leave to remain status in this country has been up in the air for quite some time. There is a six-month window that the UK Boarder Agency promises to respond within, but we did not expect to have to wait that long. Since sending off all of our paperwork, pictures and money to the Boarder Agency we have not heard anything… for months. Long months of hearing nothing reminds me of back in the day what it might have felt like for missionaries who travelled to far off lands only to be able to communicate through letters that took months to reach distant shores. It must have felt like they were cast aside, out of sight, out of mind.

As our last blog entry said, we engaged our church family into our situation, we invited them to stand with us to pray that we'd get the visa, get the passports, be able to travel to the US, be able to carry on with the adoption process and, ultimately, continue living here without immigration issues. At the very end of the meeting on the Sunday, a man in our congregation suggested to me to contact our MP, Sir George Young. I thought that was an interesting idea and most likely one from God. I ran it past a couple other people who also thought it a good plan too, so on the Monday, I sent an email to him, not sure of what it would elicit but it certainly could not hurt.

By the Friday, we had a letter from Parliament, signed by Sir Young, stating that he was doing all that he could for our situation. This blew us away, here we are simply residents (not even legal for long-term) and he, who was in a higher place, was working on our behalf. It doesn't take a clever theologian to see the analogy there; we humans calling on Jesus, who is infinitely higher than we are in all ways, working on our behalf. He is seated at the right hand of God interceding on our behalf, on your behalf. Anyway, it was great to know that we had someone higher working behind the scenes.

Fast forward to today, and just about an hour ago, the doorbell rang. My heart raced. Rebecca leapt up to answer it. I heard an unfamiliar voice and then Rebecca say, 'OK'. A bit more silence and then she bound into the room with an envelope that looked much like the one we have been eagerly awaiting. There they were – our passports, other documents and a formal letter stating that our approved residence permits would be in our possession within 7 working days. Still a bit of watching for the postman… but bigger news just happened...our residence permits were just delivered by a jolly bald man! He didn't realize what he was giving us. We had big smiles, he then had big smiles :) Being able to connect with someone higher is amazing and knowing that the Lord hears our prayers is about as comforting as it gets.

Chapter 19

December 2013 – January 2014

The relief of our paperwork returning meant that we could in fact take our planned trip to the United States, hopefully our last for quite some time. It was not the easiest trip west as we had a remarkable change taking place in our lives at home and here we were once again answering the questions about adoption.

Blog Post: 19th December 2013 – Reflections from this vantage point

It is two years now since we embarked upon the journey of adoption, and ours has spanned both the American scene and now the British one too. It seems like a short amount of time compared to the 23 more years needed in order to catch Abraham and Sarah in the amount of time waiting for their promised child. It happened again while on our America trip in November that somebody prayed over us and felt that we were like Abraham and Sarah. I have now lost track of the number of times and places where we have been encouraged in that way. While they went through such difficulty in moving from their homeland, had to pick up their belongings and tents numerous times, had to wait for years for promises of God, all did come to pass. They faced much trial and testing, but as Rebecca spoke of in Goshen a couple of weeks ago, there is a price which follows the promises.

If you would have said to us a couple years back that at the end of 2013 and the dawn of 2014 that we would be awaiting a couple more meetings with our social worker in this country and looking forward to a panel meeting in the new year we would be quite surprised. Just two short years ago, we were eagerly filling in applications and forms to do with the process in Indiana. At this point, we had booked tickets for our month-long adventure of February 2012. We didn't know what to expect, only that we knew we were on the right path, and that was a winding one, sometimes hardly paved with clarity. A good friend, who we love and trust, once shared with Rebecca to 'enjoy the view while we travel down this road, there is much to see if we look up'. How often do you and I miss the intricate and beautiful details of nature because we are staring at the path, or miss the interesting animals scurrying around, because we are fixated on the path and not the surroundings.

Our drive back to Indiana from New York, just a couple of weeks ago, was gorgeous. Fresh lake-effect snow blanketed an area which took at least 4 hours to drive through. The roads were clear with a snowflake in the air from time to time and hardly any traffic, so gazing around was not difficult. It was for the most part a crisp sunny morning and still enough that the snow had not melted off the trees or been blown about. It was a canvas of white, one like we don't witness now living in England, and one that was so much fun to drive through and take in, while we chatted about a wonderful time in Elmira, New York. I'm thankful for those memories which could have easily been missed had we not taken in the view.

We are still gazing around us, where we have come with our adoption process in the last few months and clear pointers of how to move forward in the UK. We still love to tell the story of how God provided a house for us to live in when there was seemingly nothing around. The church family that we so love continues to grow and increasingly be a place of life, evidenced this past weekend when we threw a Family Christmas Party for the village and had over 100 people come and enjoy! We have so many people we've met and become friends with over the last year; friends who weren't there at the beginning of this journey but can join in now.

The year was turning once again. 2014 was on the cusp of the calendar. The excitement continued to build as we got further and further into this process.

Blog Post: 9th January 2014 – How Time Flies

I still can't believe it has been well over 5 years (half a decade, wow!) since we moved to England. It has been nearly 2 years since our adoption prep trip to Indiana. It's been close to a year since the watershed conversations that led us to inspect the adoption process in this country and abandon the one in the States. My how time flies!

The beginning of a new year brings with it new hopes, dreams and plans for the coming days. In our case, there are some really exciting thoughts that we hold onto, coming into 2014. Some specifics about our process, which we have not expressed are the following (sorry this seems a bit clinical but I want to express the process as clearly as possible):

- We have almost completed our homestudy process, meaning that we are finished with the interview process that was done by our social worker. A profile report needs to be done based on these interviews. These were great times together, we really appreciate our worker and the depth with which we had conversation.

- We are scheduled to go to 'panel' in the middle of March. The panel is a group of people who are knowledgeable about the adoption process and they gather to hear the 'case' of prospective adopting couples. After reading the case profile, they meet to ask questions of our social worker and ourselves. Provided that there is nothing unforeseen, we are then approved to adopt.
- Either right before or right after the panel, we'll receive profiles of waiting children from our agency. It's then time for us to look through them; determine which ones we feel drawn to, and then seek further information. This part can take a very short amount of time depending on how quickly we decide and how many profiles come our way.
- Once the child is narrowed down to one, there is a matching panel, where we as adopters would be approved specifically for that one profile and then a date is set to meet the child, and eventually have the child in our home.

Speaking of timing, I would say that we have learned to wait as this has not been a 100-meter sprint, but much more like a 1500-meter race. To us the timings are all the Lord's. He has been the one leading our way the whole way. Our own plans and timings were blown out of the water long ago. As a result, we are not all that concerned about how fast or slow certain parts of this process might take. We are aware of a couple adopting who were just recently approved and are already going to the 'matching panel' for that child. It has happened oh so quickly. That could happen in our case too, or maybe not, maybe it will linger on, either way we are prepared to be on God's programme not our own.

The above list is just that, a list, but one that we knew would ultimately lead us into huge life changes. There was some trepidation as we thought about how much there was to do but again we had already experienced many difficult situations and feelings during our process. Life can be viewed from various perspectives, what one might find difficult may be a breeze to the next person. I can build hardly anything but have friends who can put anything together with or without instructions. It's all about how we see things.

Blog Post: 28th January 2014 – -11 F, it's all relative

So here I am, sitting in a coffee shop in Oakley, sipping a frothy cappuccino and catching up on the news of the day online. At first there was nobody in the shop and then a group of three ladies came in and sat down close to where I am perched in the corner. Just as I was on the WNDU news site from Northern Indiana and reading that the air temps are -11 degrees Fahrenheit, the ladies next to me start talking about the weather: "This month has been so bad, it hasn't been that cold, but it has been a really bad month." I found this interesting. While it is true that there has been bucketfuls of rain, it hasn't even sniffed the freezing point. I'll bet our friends in Indiana would be more than happy to approach the freezing point.

Rebecca and I were talking the other day and she recognized that if we had not been able to travel in November then we'd be snowbound along with everyone else in Goshen during these weeks. It's all relative, isn't it? What is 'bad' here and 'not too cold' would be welcome with a red carpet somewhere else. We are so thankful that we were able to see all our friends/family while in the US in November and without any hiccups, no travel warnings or snow removal needed.

Yesterday, somebody asked Rebecca 'Is there anything that you want to do before the adoption goes through?' Her answer was 'no, not really'. We have been able to live life to the fullest, to travel to many a distant land, to attend so many great games/concerts/shows, to live in two countries, to have amazing jobs with great co-workers, all of this to name just a bit of the life that Lord has had us lead. Wow what a fun, life-giving time we have had and do have daily. There is no reason to expect that to change. What we do day-to-day will change, probably a few less strategy board games, not as many late nights watching basketball, more visits to kid friendly places that for a long time we have not wanted or needed to frequent.

Are we up for these changes (obviously there are loads more too)? I'd say we are. It's all relative. I heard a couple not too long ago say that they had a great time on their first night out without kids in three years. We've had nights out for 17+ years anytime we wanted, responsibilities permitting, of course. We look forward to the days coming where we actually *have to* stay in, not just because we decide to, we have to. There may not be a sitter or maybe a little one is not feeling too well, or simply needs some special time. To some that might sound like an unfortunate change of plans or a downer that 'freedom' is now gone, we'll take it, we've been 'free' for a while. Again, it's all relative to your situation.

We're excited that some of the other people who were going through training here in July with us have now been approved to adopt. One has a little girl coming home in March; two others go to panel tomorrow; others did a fortnight ago. It's all happening. For us, the next big date comes in March at some point, and then we'll see from there. Another thing that is relative is waiting. We've all been there, whether it is waiting for a parcel, an update on a loved-one's health or for a bus that is running late. Sometimes the waiting is quite simple, other times, depending on the situation, it can be excruciating. For us, we've been in this game long enough to know that good things come to those who wait.

Chapter 20

He is Called Jesus
The Only Begotten

Take some time to create a list (either in your head or on paper) of extremely famous people, people who transcend cultures and ages on earth who will most likely still be known a millennium from now as they are today. That list might include political figures like Alexander the Great, Winston Churchill and Martin Luther King who fought for others or Einstein and Marie Curie who advanced the world scientifically. Maybe you'd include Mozart, Cleopatra, Plato, da Vinci, Hitler and Shakespeare. This list could carry on. However, in reality, there are not a vast number of 'world changers' who either have lived or are a part of the 6.5 billion on earth presently. A name that encapsulates the above list and would likely make the list of most (certainly in the Western World) is Jesus Christ, the only begotten Son of God.

Away in a manger, What Child is This, Infant Lowly - each of these Christmas songs evokes images of a newborn wiggling around a feeding trough laid with straw. This little body wrapped in swaddling clothes born into the grim political and cultural situation of the Jewish people who were once again an oppressed people, this time by the Romans who dominated the known world at the time. This little infant king had been prophesied and foretold of for many centuries. In addition, a whole nation of people had been waiting for their Messiah; as the song says, 'My

Deliverer is coming, My Deliverer is standing by'. The magi from Eastern countries had ventured by caravan via trade routes for possibly thousands of miles to meet the young monarch.

Some shepherds had done the unthinkable; they had abandoned their flocks to race into town to see the starlit one. Shepherds were one of, if not, the lowest rung on the social ladder. They were probably children or older folks who were sent to the fields to tend the sheep. Did they keep quiet about their excitement of a Saviour being born? You can imagine that they excitedly told numerous others that a Savior had been born. Most likely the townspeople and other shepherds they told were surprised, in awe and asking important questions like: is he just a newborn? Who are his parents? Why is he so special? Did you say a group of angels told you about him? I'm sure there were other enquiries as well as you can imagine their disbelief. It seems as though the joy struck shepherds didn't have the same line of questioning as they carried on rejoicing and praising God for all they had seen and heard. They had seen with their eyes, had heard the cries of the infant and had probably talked with his mom and dad. Can you imagine what that first conversation would have been like? Maybe something like this:

Shepherd: *(to each other)* Hey guys, over here, I think this is it, the star seems to be right above this cave, and I think I hear the cry of a little one.

Shepherd: *(to Joseph and Mary)* I know this is so weird but tonight a group of angels came to our hillside to speak and sing about a Savior being born here in Bethlehem. They

said to follow the star and it led us here. Is that a newborn baby cry that we hear? It sounds crazy but is He the Saviour they talked about? If not, then we'll get outta here and we're really sorry...

Joseph: You're right, we arrived here yesterday and this little stable was all we could find. The town is manic with the census taking place. He was born just a couple of hours ago.

Shepherd: What did the angels mean by 'He is a Saviour'? He is cute, resting there in the straw, but why is he so special?

Mary: Well those are great questions, he is so very special to us

Shepherd: You both must be so proud. He looks so peaceful; do you think he looks more like dad or mom?

Joseph: Of course, we are proud. He does carry a peace unlike other babes. We think he looks like Mary mostly.

Shepherd: I can see that but from this angle he definitely has your chin and cheekbones Joseph. It is Joseph, right?

Joseph: Yes, it is Joseph. I don't think that his features are that defined, really we are overjoyed to have a healthy baby and being born here in this little barn, of all places.

Shepherd: What a story dad. You are both amazing - with the long travel down here to Bethlehem and being able to find this place with all the hubbub in the city.

Joseph: Feel free to carry on admiring him. I think that Mary is going to attempt to get some much-needed rest but do stay here in the straw as long as you like.

Shepherd: Thanks Joseph, you do make a wonderful father already.

A Picture of Fatherhood

Admittedly, the above script is a fictional take on the dialogue, but it is accurate that Joseph had to face questions about his fatherhood. In the culture of 1st Century Palestine, the idea of an unmarried couple giving birth was grounds for possible death or, at least, unending questions of parental legitimacy. To put yourself in the shoes of Joseph would be walking through scorn and unacceptance from most, but also intense devotion to the woman he loved and the firstborn who he so adored.

The Messiah, Christ, was to come through the line of David and that line is what passed through Joseph. Jesus, although not blood relation to Joseph, was in the line, genealogy and ancestry of David that eventually extended to Joseph. The adoption of Jesus into the family of Joseph was so authentic, complete and genuine that the fatherhood of Joseph was not questioned in the scriptures. The likes of David, Solomon, Rahab, Ruth, Jesse and many more generations passed on through Joseph to Jesus and into the prophetic realization of the Messiah.

Fatherhood is not merely about an infant who needs feeding, changing and laid down for a nap. It is about the relationship with the child, as he or she matures. What must this have been like for Joseph, his son, perfect, sinless and yet still a toddler and an excited little boy? He was a little boy learning the carpentry trade from his father; a boy who quickly turned into an impeccable young man. We actually don't have much record of how Joseph raised Jesus other than the interaction at the temple in Luke 2:41-52. At this time, Joseph and Mary had left to go home, along with the large group who had come to Jerusalem for a Passover feast. While journeying they realized that Jesus was not among the crowd; where was he? In the temple. He was speaking with the elders and priests, asking questions and the Bible says they were amazed with his knowledge and answers. His parents did not get upset with him, they found him, asked him to come along and he gladly did.

In addition to the lack of detail about the parenthood style and stories from these formative years, we also don't know what Jesus called Joseph: Dad, Pop, Father, Papi? Who knows? What we do know is that Jesus called his heavenly father, Abba.

Abba Father

Abba is a term of endearment. It meant 'daddy' and was an intimate name for the father. Growing up as a little boy, I usually called my parents mommy and daddy; especially when I wanted something special. This term, Abba, is a special term and a loving word for a parent. Abba was not a name used for God until Jesus used it. In the Old Testament, God is spoken of and spoken to by various names, including Yahweh, El, and God of Israel, to name a few.

He was not called Father and, certainly not as personal a reference, Abba. Many people spoke to God and heard from God but were not as familiar as to use the term 'daddy'. The term was often heard as a name in the Aramaic household, but not in relationship to God in Judaism. Jesus using this term Abba shows the special relationship he holds with God, the Father of creation and the Father of lights.

Our Father in Heaven

When asked by the disciples how they should pray, Jesus responded with probably the most famous prayer of them all: “Our Father who art in heaven…”. He started the instructive prayer with ‘Our Father’; he invited them to join with his sonship in reference to God. This is no small statement. In the Old Testament, there were the children of Israel, fearers of God, even men and women appointed by God, but not people who were called sons and daughters of God. Genesis 6:1 actually refers to angels when saying ‘sons of God’. The disciples and all those who were present at the sermon on the mount were privy to the amazing proclamation that they can and are encouraged to address our Father; not some far off being but one who is intimately involved in their lives.

This is still true for us today as we pray to ‘Our Father’. God is intricately involved in my life, just as Clifton, my father, has been for the 43 years of my life. What an invitation we are afforded to address the creator of the cosmos, the Alpha and Omega as Father, Papa or Daddy!

Jesus was the prototype of this relationship of son and Father. He was Joseph’s son and clearly God’s only begotten son, as well. There are references in the gospels to paternal-child situation this one coming from John 1:11-12:

'But as many as received Him, to them He gave the right to become children of God, even to those who believe in His name, who were born, not of blood nor of the will of the flesh nor of the will of man, but of God.'

Later in the New Testament, the apostle Paul extends this father-son/daughter motif further into our lives. Writing to the believers in the Greek city of Corinth he said in 2 Corinthians 6:18:

And I will be a father to you. And you shall be sons and daughters to Me," Says the Lord Almighty.

Do you think that Mary and Joseph thought about the ramifications on history and the world-changing son they raised? Did they expect that he would most likely top lists in the 'most remembered', 'written about' and 'important people' in human history? If they hadn't contemplated that possibility, they would have to reckon with thoughts and expectations of their son when they encountered Simeon who was a holy man in the temple. This happened on the 8th day after Jesus was born, the customary day for circumcision of young Jewish boys. Joseph and Mary took newborn Jesus to the temple and heard the following statements about him:

**Luke 2:29-35 – "Sovereign Lord, as you have promised,
you may now dismiss-your servant in peace. 30 For my eyes
have seen your salvation, 31 which you have prepared in
the sight of all nations: 32 a light for revelation to the
Gentiles, and the glory of your people Israel."**

**33 The child's father and mother marvelled at what was
said about him. 34 Then Simeon blessed them and said to**

Mary, his mother: "This child is destined to cause the falling and rising of many in Israel, and to be a sign that will be spoken against, [35] so that the thoughts of many hearts will be revealed. And a sword will pierce your own soul too."

Talk about being proud of your son: 'salvation in his eyes', 'a light for revelation', cause the rise and fall of many', 'hearts revealed and the piercing of their souls too'. What an amazing variety of statements to say about an 8-day old? If that wasn't enough, the prophetess Anna who had not left the temple for years, praying day and night, said that this babe was the 'redemption of Jerusalem'. There was nothing more the Jews wanted than the redemption of their holy city. They had waited for hundreds of years to experience freedom in Jerusalem, waiting for a saviour to rescue the people. They were pining and hoping for the redemption of their land and the prophetess Anna foretold that baby Jesus would be that person.

John 1:14 says that Jesus became one of us and made his dwelling among us. As Peterson says in the Message, he moved into the neighbourhood, an adopted baby, a perfect boy then man, the Son of God, the Son of Joseph, this is Jesus our example of who and how God is. He was the picture of adoption personified, the image of the invisible God.

Joseph faced scrutiny for his decision to stand by Mary, but he did not waver after hearing from God about this soon to be born baby. Joseph was a carpenter, he taught his son the trade, he provided for him and provided a future for him in the family business. Joseph was the picture of how a non-biological father can be introduced to a life and be the consistent rock for a child.

Chapter 21

February – March 2014

As the homestudy part of the process came to an end, we looked forward to the next set of meetings. So much has happened over the last three years, I attempted to put it all in one entry during the latter part of February 2014.

Blog Post: 20th February 2014 – Interviews, forms, home-study complete... now what?

For those of you who have followed our journey of adoption, you'll know that there have been many twists and turns along the way. (If you have followed along you might find this redundant, if you haven't, here is a whistle-stop tour of our journey.)

It was exactly two years ago that we were in Northern Indiana going back and forth to Indy for meetings and heading over to the agency offices which were about an hour-half drive to Kouts, for interviews.

Shortly after that trip, we were approved to adopt from America but then over the course of the next year, we never received 'the call'. The one stating that there was a mother ready to give us her child. This did come as a surprise to us. At the time, we expected to be uprooted for a couple of months while traveling back to the US to meet and care for a newborn. After being in the US, we'd then come back to England to carry on with life as a family, but this is not the way that it has worked for us. It's about a year ago now that we recognised we could adopt from this country. In fact, there is, at present, a push for more Christians to adopt. We didn't even know it was an option until sitting in meetings last Feb at a leaders' conference. Those couple of days 'up north' really did change our thinking.

Now here we are, a year on from that understanding. We've dropped out of using the agency in America to adopt. We've gone through training, interviews, home study, references and all the detail needed to adopt here. We've moved in the last six months to a smaller home, miraculously had our leave-to-remain visas come through the post and did our much-anticipated trip to the US in November. It has been a time of transition. Well, now we have another date to be excited about... in less than one month from now we go to our adoption panel meeting.

The panel meeting is essentially where we can be approved to adopt in this country. From that date onwards, we will receive profiles of kids through email. There are many children who are available to adopt; one of our jobs is to consider which ones we'd like to move forward with and then narrow that number down to where contact is made with their social worker. This is an exciting aspect of the journey as for us it will be the first time that we actually will be doing something other than waiting, interviewing or filling in forms. We'll be looking at children and their profiles. To some extent that ball is in our court, usually in this process it isn't, but while choosing profiles of children, it is. From there other hurdles may arise but for now we are excited as the report our social worker does is finished and the interviews and form filling are complete...onward to the next step.

If you are looking for ways to pray for us, it's usually about timing and patience, so pray for the timing of God with our approval and patience for us as we carry on down this road. We are so grateful for all those who have journeyed with us, and for all of those who have lifted prayers on our behalf.

After the tediousness of form filling and interviews comes the important decision-making meetings. We were excited about this part of the process. After all, it all has to be done in order to reach the goal of children in the home.

In the days before the panel meeting, it was all that was on our mind. We were expectant and had faith that this part of the story was coming to a close.

Blog Post: 16th March 2014 - Run up to the Big Day

I have been asked various times in the last couple of weeks, 'what are you thankful for in the last week?' Each time my mind has gone to the forthcoming panel meeting. Various aspects of being thankful for the panel meeting, one of those being that it has been on our hearts but not on our minds. That saying has become a key factor in our daily lives, if not across the whole adoption process. With the coming panel day, if the 'what if's' were consistently on our minds it would be too much to handle. They are rather on our hearts, prayerfully considered, with many, many, many others standing with us.

One positive about us, a prospective adoptive couple, is our wide network. It has been something that our social worker has stated many times. To us it is normal to have throngs who are interested, ask questions, pray in the background, pray in the foreground and, generally, are involved in our lives. It means that the run-up to the big day of the panel meeting is not one that we are doing alone. Knowing that we are not alone, that the Holy

Spirit is with us daily and our friends/family around the world walking with us, actually it is more running with us, in the lead up to the big day...the excitement and hope that lies around the 19th of March...The unknown future that holds so much possibility for our family as it grows into who God has prepared it to be.

The day of the panel meeting was finally here: two homestudy processes, two countries, trainings, travel, visas, ups and downs all done and we were at the 19th.

Blog Post: 19th March 2014 - Panel Day, parts 1,2,3

Part 1

Today is a day unlike no other (every day is, but you get my drift), it is an incredibly special one for the two of us. Our date with 12 people we've never seen before; 12 people we'll probably never see again, but 12 people who have a say in our future plans. I'll bet it feels a bit like going before a jury, (I've never done that) knowing that in a few hours you'll be standing in front of a group of people whose job it is to analyze and draw conclusions.

Part 2

What is the deal with waiting areas that are either sterile, have no reading materials, music source or even art on the wall? It does not make it any easier to pass time when there aren't any magazines to flip through, some music to hum along to or something on the wall to stare at. So be it, there we were waiting in a room we had frequented many times before during training, this time waiting to be called into the chamber on the other side of the wall. We sort of knew what awaits us, a horseshoe shaped grouping of tables with two chairs at the open end, they were going to be ours.

Our social worker was in the waiting room with us, she is fabulous, really on our side, a true advocate. We can't say enough about her abilities, her understanding of the process, but ultimately about her care for us. We also were able to meet her manager who we had spoken with on the phone, so there the four of us sat.

The protocol is for the social workers to go into the panel meeting to discuss our situation. This means anything from answering questions, giving clarity or pointing people to the corresponding portion of the report. This is not an easy job, in some respects at this point it is like the role of an attorney, bringing out our case and answering how we would. Usually after a few minutes, the ones who are adopting are brought in and asked a couple of clarifying questions.

That is how it is usually done, if you know us you'll know that we don't end up doing the 'usual' very often. That's not by choice, one of our great friends in the UK says that 'we don't do things by halves'.

Time goes by slowly sometimes. When you are anxious and unsure of when you might be called in, whether it be an interview or the doctor's office, it's an example of the clock moving at turtle-like-speed. This was our case. The white-walled room, us sitting there, mobiles turned off so we were ready, again simply sitting there. We chatted as much as you can. We prayed again as much as one can. We simply sat there. At about 12:10 or so after being there for some 40 minutes, we decided that praying was what we needed to press into.

After maybe 5 minutes or so of really digging in, a peace came upon the room, one that Rebecca felt and at the point we knew that we were ready, the path had been paved. What we were to find out post panel meeting was at about that time they were unsure if we were going to be called in at all. The waiting did continue for another 10 minutes or so, these were more manageable for our emotions. Then, the manager appeared and said that they were almost ready for us. Another 5 minutes later, she, our social worker and the lead panel member came into our room. We were invited in to the actual meeting.

I'd have to say that we were ready, there were some questions they pointed our way. We did our best to answer, our social worker had covered our situation very well, she had tied up our case very tightly. After about 10 minutes of answering their enquiries, we resorted back to our familiar waiting room.

Part 3

This is quite short. After another few minutes of not knowing, the lead person on the panel came and spoke with us. It was immense GREAT NEWS that we were approved by the panel, but, (and a big but) another person in the organisation has to officially sign off on the approval first. Being approved was huge news and all of us celebrated quietly in the little white room. From there we simply exited and enjoyed lunch and shopping together.

Although we had been approved, we still needed to wait for the for the official sign off of approval before we could move forward with seeing any profiles. Essentially, we were left with a 'yes' but had to wait a bit longer for the official decision. While some on the panel thought we would be great parents, others did not think so, for particular reasons which I will not go in to detail here.

It is confusing, but on the day of the meeting, we were reassured by our social worker that approval would be given. It did, however, need to be signed off by the head manager of the agency. Again we were told not to worry as this sometimes happens and that the agency decision maker would come to a conclusion quickly (and hopefully a positive one!) over this matter.

Blog Post: 26th March 2014 - And so we wait

Maybe 1 in 4 entries on this blog is about waiting, maybe less, but it feels like at least a quarter. We have put our time in over the last 2 1/2 years since our first enquiry in Sept 2011. We have in fact waited for phone calls back, emails to come through, paperwork to be mailed, meetings to be set, airplanes to take off, important dates to arrive and so on. What the last week has felt like is at a different level.

As I write this, the famed Malaysian jet which disappeared somewhere into the Southern Hemisphere has not been found, they still can't say with 100% surety where the crash took place; whether a crash took place; what happened to the passengers and why this jet traversed so far off the given flight path. To the family and friends of the numerous passengers, the wait for news at this point, whether good or bad, must be excruciating. They simply don't know. They are in a place of scared wonder, knowing that hearing nothing is as good as the worst news they could hear. Waiting for much anticipated updates and news is difficult in the best of times and nearly impossible in the worst of times.

I am not intending to compare our situation to the horrific disappearance of the Malaysian jetliner, ours is not life and death in that sense. We have found ourselves in another intense space of waiting, eagerly expecting a phone call/email, some kind of contact from the adoption agency. In some respects, the panel meeting feels like weeks ago and, at the same time, it feels like a few minutes ago we were sitting, praying and waiting in the room on the other side of the wall. We understand in hind-sight the power of prayer happening during our meeting, the shifting of the panel members thoughts of who we were. We didn't realise it at the time but all changed after the intense prayer that took place at about 12:05pm.

Following the great news that the panel had approved us, we were so relieved, but there was a caveat. There needed to be a sign-off from one other person before it could be official. This did not sound like it would be a radically difficult part of the process, a phone call or a meeting at most, and then it's full steam ahead. In fact, here we are, a week later still awaiting the affirming phone call, the one that says 'yes' and congrats on this part of the journey being finished.

It's raw. We've been with other people in the raw. We've seen heartache of crushing news. We've seen the massive disappointment of parents not doing their job of being the adults. We've sat and prayed with folks as they were the ones crying tears of sadness and frustration. In that respect, we understand the raw, but that doesn't make it any easier in the present day.

There continued to be no news sadly. Although, we did a get a phone call.

Blog Post: 31st March 2014 - Deflation

Inflation is a word used in commerce and it is used when blowing up a balloon or filling something with air. The opposite of that is deflation, like when the blown-up balloon hasn't been tied yet and then it rapidly shoots the air all over as it flies all over when let go. The balloon deflates quickly and quite out of control. As much as we wanted to hear a 'yes', as much as we desired to have this portion of the journey over, we had to endure another deflating phone call.

This one came late on Monday afternoon after I had been trying very unsuccessfully to pound a ground spike into our back garden. I was flustered after realising that the clothesline pole didn't fit into the spike, and then to make matters worse, I found a way to accidently jam a plastic cylinder into the spike as well, meaning that it now couldn't work as the pole wouldn't go in hardly at all. If you know me, you know that D, I and Y are not in the name Earl. So, I was already really bothered when a call we had hoped would come, came!

I gave up on the ground spike debacle and followed Rebecca to the front-room where the conversation was moved to speaker phone. There wasn't really good or really bad news that the man from the agency shared, it was deflating though. Basically, the person who needs to look more at the forms we had efficiently emailed on the previous Friday was not around this week; she's on holiday. I thought something like this might happen, we do all that we can, and then because a particular person is on holiday, our timetable is changed. Of course, there is nothing practically that we can do about it. We simply have to accept it and carry on.

Maybe it is all down to the timing of God and when we do get a firm approval the timing will be just right for the right child. Maybe we are to learn something in the waiting, even though so close to this finish line. Probably it is a combo of both and more, but that does not make it easy to stomach. Yes, deflating but we'll carry on, that's what we do.

Chapter 22

April 2014

The whole of March was a blur, there was no quick decision, in fact a decision was not taken at all, and April arrived. Having to answer the never-ending question of 'when?' seemed unbearable. Those close to us knew that we were cracking. We could not sustain the 'happy face' much longer, but it did feel as though the end was drawing near, in a good way.

Blog Post: 8th April 2014 – God's Timing

When somebody is coming up to a significant birthday milestone, like 40, for example, taking stock in life is quite a normal activity. I have to say that I've been doing that, but in the midst of a coming party on Saturday, celebrations on Monday and getting cards from people a dark shadow continues to hang. As of this writing we are still unclear of our status as adopting parents. We have not been given the firm go-ahead and the agency has not asked for anything more which would indicate that they have all they need to make decisions. This is both comforting and concerning. If they do in fact have it all, then why the delay? If they don't have everything, then what else will be enquired about? What other forms may we have to produce?

Unfortunately, too often when times are difficult, the response of well-wishing people (usually Christians) comes across as trite. This happens all the time at funerals and when really rough news about a person's health or financial situation comes into the light. Often it is said, 'it's God's timing' or 'He works everything out for good' and while these may be true that doesn't mean that they are easy to stomach. Again, we have to remind ourselves that we are not waiting on the news of a loved son in the military who has gone 'missing in action' or to find out if the delicate brain surgery was successful or not. We recognise it is not a life and death situation that we wait on tenterhooks for, but that does not mean that swallowing the pill of 'It's God's timing, and His is always best' is very easy or comfortable.

Of course, our thinking could change, and very dramatically in a short space of time, once we get that important phone call. Until then the protocol is to keep the mobile handy, have it charged and always turned on, even the sound on, not just on vibrate mode.

There were a large number of blog entries during this week. We were reaching the point of worry rather than faith and that is a scary place to be. At this point, penning my thoughts was about all I could do. In truth, we were distraught.

Blog Post: 10th April 2014 – Did you send that email?

I don't remember the first time I sent or received an email. I suppose it was 11 years ago when my account at Hotmail was set up with ETPR29 as the name – my nickname given by the youth group guys, 'ETP', my surname initial, followed by my age. My how much has changed. Now, hardly a half-hour goes by without an email coming in or being sent out. How often is an email received with an expectation of a response immediately or at least within the day? Long live the days of the letter where it travelled to its destination or even the phone call. Now it's all pinged off on in an email (or message, twitter etc...) It is all so immediate and instant.

How ironic, with the waiting game that we've been playing, that it seems like what we are waiting on now is an email. A person at the agency to send another person at the agency an email. Once that little piece of communication takes place we can move forward to the final step of our approval process. It feels like it's been months since our panel meeting; actually, it has been 3 weeks. At times we've been really relaxed, like last week when we knew that the holiday of one of the contacts superseded our process. Or even the first couple of days, when we simply did not expect a quick response.

This week has not been as easy, more or less with mobiles pinned to our hips waiting for the ring-tone to go off with the agency on the other end of the line. That's the way yesterday was, in town all day, hoping that I hadn't missed the call with all the sounds of the shopping district and traffic. As a result of the concern, I was checking the mobile incessantly usually to find an email that had come in, but not a missed call. Today, we actually made a call rather than waiting on one. It was exceedingly helpful, even if only for our own psyche. We'll see about tomorrow or even later today, maybe a phone call or an email will arrive in the inbox.

Blog Post: 11th April 2014 – Is Today the Day?

You probably remember asking that question as a little kid when you were excited about going on vacation or a visit from family members. 'Is today the day we go?' It's fraught with anticipation, but also the unsurety of the happenings of the day. That's us. We are in that same place as most 4-year olds before the car is packed and the journey begins. We had some marginally good news yesterday; we have been promised a phone call today, but not sure what will be said on the other end. We have reason to believe that our approval will be granted, and that it might be today, but we can't be for sure.

There isn't much we can be sure of; Ben Franklin famously said there are two things you can count on... death and taxes. He's mostly right. You can count on those, but I think there are more than those; one is the love of the Lord Jesus Christ throughout all of life's ups and downs and another one of those is change. Change is always happening, around us and to us, maybe I'm thinking this way as I encroach further on being 40, being 'over the hill' as they say. It used to be life began after 40, now its life begins after 60, if that's the case I'm still a toddler.

Rebecca and I have had our fair share of change, I suppose all married couples do: we've moved house, found new jobs, gone back to Uni, sold our possessions, moved to a new continent, gone to Bible school, lived with various people, started a new profession here, on and on it goes. We've been told that we're good at change…whatever that means, I'm not sure. That we can adapt and do it quickly, again that is probably a really helpful skill, but I might not want to use it as often as I do :)

Blog Post: 12th April 2014 – Bordering on the Absurd

Yesterday, near the end of another day which brought us no further news, I uttered a statement that our situation was getting absurd and that it means there must be a much greater reason for our waiting. In essence, we are waiting on an email. It's already been agreed; it's been requested three times, but with still no answer. Can we understand this? Nope. Do we usually respond to emails immediately? Yup. Does that change our situation presently and how we do things? It doesn't unfortunately.

We have some really trustworthy and great people working on our behalf, some real advocates who are fighting our corner. As I sit here thinking about Palm Sunday tomorrow it does seem absurd but so did the Saviour of the world riding into Jerusalem aboard a lowly donkey, not a war horse, coming in as a meagre peasant, not a conquering hero adorned with medals. There are examples of absurdity all throughout the Bible, God has a way of using the absurd to get across the point of his power and plan, we're blessed to be part of that in our situation.

My 40th, a day that I'll not soon forget, probably most people remember that special day. For us it was tough, sure we went out to celebrate with a meal, shopping and a bit of a road trip. However, it did feel like a haze, as though we were going through the motions.

Blog Post: 14th April 2014 – Anticipation for Who Knows What

There are not that many days when you roll out of bed after a night of slumber and have no clue what the next day holds. It is a rarity in our society of intricately planned-out diaries to have space, let alone a whole day where you don't know what will be taking place. For those of you who don't know, today is my 40th birthday and along with the unknown of what the 40s will bring, there is the immediacy of 'What does Rebecca have up her sleeve?' We both are quite good at planning special birthdays for each other, usually involving secrets. Even though we share an email account, we find ways to plan in secret.

Anticipation and reflection have been something I've been doing a lot of lately. Last night, Lizzie asked me what were three events over the last decade that sprung to mind. If you have not tried choosing just three events from a decade, have a go! It's not that easy. It was really helpful to think back through and try to determine which ones had the most impact or were a vivid memory. In addition to reflecting, there is also the anticipating that comes along with a birthday and, on this occasion, a special one with a '0'.

It feels like Rebecca and I are consistently waiting; another perspective could be that it is 'anticipating'. Is that a lighter spin on waiting? Does anticipating, rather than frustratingly waiting, take away the life-lessons of patience and long-suffering? In jobs past, I have been accused of being overly positive. Is that really a bad thing? I suppose looking at the glass half full, the silver lining is my m/o. Along with that look at life, comes the joy of anticipating, recognising that there is great stuff on the way, fun times and special occasions with special people.

Of course, with all the waiting that we've been doing with the adoption process (31 months from start time in Sept 2011), we have also had plenty of time to anticipate. We can't really plan but that is different from the excitement of anticipating what might be, how many children will we adopt, boy or girl, age of the child or children – so much to look forward to. That is where we are presently, in a space of looking forward and seeing what the next day brings us.

I wrote two entries in one day, on my birthday no less. Read the second and you can probably sense the frustration.

Blog Post: 14th April 2014 – Tomorrow, Tomorrow

I'm not a big fan of the musical Annie. I love musicals but for some reason have never gotten into that one. Surprising, since it is the story of a little orphan girl who is taken in and finds a new life, but I haven't. I really like others, like Les Mis, Billy Elliot and Wicked to name a few. Anyway, the song 'Tomorrow' from Annie is incredibly well known and even I know that one, the promise of tomorrow only being a day away. That is where we find ourselves now in the adoption marathon, tomorrow looks to be the day of the decision. Will we be fully approved and moving on to the next stage of seeing profiles of children waiting to be adopted? It looks promising that tomorrow the decision will be reached.

We have learned long ago that depending on dates as promises are a foolhardy action, but that does not mean we can't be excited. There is always that possibility that the meeting doesn't happen or the right person happened to be out of the office, again all out of our control. What we can control is the ability to pray, to put our hope in the Lord Jesus and to continue riding this crazy rollercoaster of getting through the adoption process. Does it make sense to put many hopes and dreams on one day? Probably not, in the course of a life it is a very small amount, but wow does it feel long when you're awaiting a decision. I've been in that place before. You've probably been in that place before of knowing you gave a good interview but will you be chosen for the job? It can be so difficult to let the hours slip by, but what other choice is there? So tomorrow, tomorrow you're only a day away!

You are probably expecting to read about some good news soon. It seemed as though we had been through the ringer for *years* after the panel meeting, in reality it was only 29 days but 29 long days. On the 17th April, it finally all changed!

Blog Post: 17th April 2014 - Long Awaited...Seal of Approval

4:17 pm – Thursday afternoon, I was outside pounding in the new ground spike I had purchased (what's with me, ground spikes and important calls?) and THE PHONE CALL came. There was a shriek in a good way from indoors and it was Rebecca's voice giving away the results of the phone call. We've been ready by the mobile now for 4 weeks, since the 19th of March. On the other end of Rebecca's mobile was our social worker, she had good news, no great news, make that THE NEWS we've been eagerly awaiting and praying for.

This is the seal of approval. We have been officially approved to adopt here in the UK, that part of this arduous journey has come to completion. As I have told friends, this process is like the Tour De France, it's one leg after another of a race, each one different and each one extremely intense. This last stretch was like we could see the finish line but for some reason could not cross the tape. That tape has now been crossed, that part of this journey has been passed. We now move forward.

A bit of time passed and we caught our collective breath. We'd made it this far. Using the Tour De France analogy again, we knew we weren't finished with the whole race but had completed a very difficult stage. However, there would still be plenty of pedalling and work to do as we moved toward the realisation of being dad and mom.

Blog Post: 28th April 2018 - The Next Steps

We've had many questions tossed our way: what are the next steps? What do you do now? When does a child come to you? Do you get one from the hospital? and on and on the questions have come. I'll attempt to give an overview, we'll see how it goes...

Our agency has contact with local authorities all across the UK and have access to the children who are in care and waiting for an adoptive family. Almost all of these children are in foster families, some since they were newly born and others at an older age after they were removed from their homes. Rebecca and I have been approved to adopt either 1 or 2 children up to the age of five. This means that we are eligible to adopt a sibling pair, twins or one child provided, they are under the age of five.

Essentially what happens is that we receive profiles of waiting children from our agency through email. There is a person at the agency who is a family finder and she connects waiting children profiles with people like us who are approved to adopt. These are usually short 2-4 page intros, including a picture, some family background, a few thoughts from their social worker and the child's likes/dislikes. Sometimes we get a full report on a child/children, which includes all of the family background, names of people involved in their life/lives, reasons for removal from the home, hopes and wishes of the parents and much more detail. These can be exhausting to read through, but they are very useful in deciding if a child/children is potentially a right fit for our family.

It is very weird to look through profiles of children, and to declare to ourselves and the agency that we cannot pursue them any further. By pursuing I mean that we ask for more information, we state that we are interested in our social worker making contact or of us being contacted, or of being shortlisted. If we are shortlisted for a child/children then a date of meeting their social worker would be decided upon, and a visit to our home would take place.

We have already said no to a couple of profiles. For various reasons, we knew that we could not go further with the waiting children. We are certain that the right one/ones are out there though. We have not travelled this far in the process to rush things or to get frustrated. This is part of the excitement, just very different from the American process where we would be waiting to be chosen, now we are somewhat doing the choosing.

Most days there were new profiles filling our inbox. To either wake up to new possibilities or to text each other to say 'check out your email' we were consistently dealing with faces and stories of awaiting children. To be the 'chooser' was such a role reversal from being the 'chosen'. Now rather than sitting back and hoping for a phone call or email, we were sifting through profiles of children who were waiting. There are thousands of children in the UK in that very situation, depending on age and situation they may not know they are waiting, but for many a phone call or email will change their lives.

Chapter 23

You are Called Son or Daughter
The Great Family of God

Growing up as a little boy, I watched any football, basketball, baseball or hockey game on TV; it didn't matter who was playing. From the age of five, I knew what games were on, which channel the game was broadcast on and who the best players were for each team, whether they were my Browns, Seminoles, Rangers or the detested Yankees and Fighting Irish.

During the breaks in action, there were always TV commercials and loads of them. For the most part they are aimed at men, guys who might like to drive a rough and tough pickup, buy a six pack, or find out the best place to invest their money. The ads were not slanted at kids or teenagers, so while my friends might be bombarded with going cuckoo for Cocoa Puffs, Lego and My Little Pony, I saw commercials from Chevy, EF Hutton and American Express. One ad always stuck with me: "Membership has its privileges", that was the tagline of the American Express credit card. Evidently, it suggested that this credit card is more special than any of the others, as being a member with them comes with privileges (still late fees though, I'm sure!). I think that American Express was on to something with their tagline. They realized the importance of belonging, and if somebody had an American Express card they had the privilege to spend their money in certain hotels and restaurants, when others could not. It may be hard to believe, but at that time not all credit cards were accepted by all restaurants and hotels.

Another example of belonging, that I personally experienced, was after joining the local gym. No longer did I have to queue to get through the turnstile to start working out. While others had to wait to pay, ask questions or sign forms, I simply swiped my card and carried on walking. I 'belonged' to the gym and along with that came the privilege of going in and using the equipment anytime it is open.

You Belong

Forget credit cards and gym memberships for now, because every one of us is a member of something and that is a family. Every one of us is either a son or daughter, whether we have much or no relationship with our mother, father or other family members. You were born, you are defined and there is reality that you are either a son or daughter.

I thank the Lord daily for my dad and mom. I am theirs, a member of the Robinson family. Some privileges of being in that family included having parents who were there for the tough times of adolescence: my dad volunteering at my high school, my mom's persistence of what I might become, not to mention food, shelter, clothing and other necessities so often taken for granted.

One of the most life-giving and hope-filled passages to me in the whole Bible is Psalm 68:6 where it says that God places the lonely in families. He recognizes that while we are born into a family that unit may not function as one, may not be desirable to live with or may have loved ones lost to death. The word says that He doesn't leave a child lonely, he places them in families, that's good news, membership does have its privileges.

God calls those who trust and fear Him many different titles, including beloved, dear ones or saints, for example. The most consistent and practically applicable name to us as humans is the title of 'child of God' or son and daughter. The apostle John, the beloved who walked and talked with Jesus, understood this motif of children. He addressed the readers 14 times in his first letter that they were children of the Most High. According to I John 3:1-2 we are given the right to be called children. I am the only one with the right to say that I am a child of Cliff and Della, but we all have the right to be called a child of God.

Children of God

The reality of sonship (this is non-gender specific) is

an important image developed throughout the New Testament. The numerous groups of Christ followers, in Rome were no doubt under scrutiny, a watchful eye and persecution, unlike we presently face in the West. In Paul's letter to this committed body of Christ, he used sonship as a term to connect them to God. Why sonship? Could they not be fingers of God, channels of His voice or saved ones? He could have used those metaphors, but to the struggling Christ's followers hearing and reading they were a son/daughter would bring an amazing amount of hope. Many of the people in that church were slaves or ex-slaves and to be deemed no longer a slave but a son was the gospel, which was good news.

Following Christ and giving it all for the Kingdom of God meant for some the opportunity to be part of a family. When Paul wrote in Romans 8:15 of us no longer being slaves but having the spirit of sonship, he used the Greek word *huiothesia,* which means adoption or literally being placed as a son. The ears and eyes of the Christians living in Rome would not miss this part of the message. This is front-page headline news. The hope brought by these words on a page meant that no matter their status and place in life they were adopted as a son/daughter in the great family of God.

One of the best-selling books on adoption is the Primal Wound by Verrier and while I was reading it a quote struck me. When speaking of a newborn given up for adoption, it stated, 'There is a sense of being a mistake, of having no right to exist, there is no sense of belonging in the family into which they were placed that into which they were born or in the universal schema'. These are a few phrases that for me when read do anything but engender hope. Aren't we blessed that the Bible does not declare this sense of un-belonging onto us? He does not think of us as mistakes or not having rights. We are never a mistake. We have the right to exist and absolutely belong in a family, one we are not born into but drawn into by the grace of God.

When somebody thinks of Jesus they may reflect on the miracles he performed, or the miraculous conception, even the gruesome passion of the cross, but they are unlikely to think about his siblings. Maybe we think of Peter, James, John and some of the other dozen disciples, but what about his biological brothers, the children of Joseph and Mary? What must it have been like to have the reflection of God on earth in the other cot on the floor of the bedroom? How would you convince mom or dad that 'he did it' when trying to get out of trouble? I'm sure there were numerous advantages and disadvantages of having Jesus as a brother.

Only Child

Both Rebecca and I are only children. I did not have

the experience of growing up with any brothers or sisters. Being an only child has it positives and negatives. When the vase was broken by a kicked ball, it was squarely my fault. My dad was at work so I couldn't even try to persuade mom that somebody else did it. When it came to chores, inside or outside, there was nobody to divide the work between, but on the flipside at the dinner table there was nobody else hoping for seconds or more dessert. There was always a direct line to mom or dad, whether that was help with homework or wanting to play a game, they were the only ones around. This is not unlike the relational connection we can have with our Heavenly Father, a direct line that is always able to be heard.

Being an only child also meant that there weren't other kids around to have shared experiences with in the everyday life of the home. My dad came from a large farming family where it was all hands on deck and so often I would hear him speak of this brother or that brother and the exploits of living on the farm. He had many shared experiences with them all; they were a group of nine brothers and one sister intertwined between them. Maybe if I had grown up with siblings, this idea of brothers together in something would have deeper meaning. By no means do I regret being an only child and it wasn't my decision to make anyway.

Brothers and Sisters

I do have an understanding of being brothers in Christ. If it is accurate that we are sons and daughters in the great family of God, then it must be true that we are brothers and sisters together in this very family. The writer of Hebrews encouraged his listeners and readers that Jesus had to be made like us and be one of the brothers, one who truly understood humanity. As Peterson so vividly put it in the message 'Jesus moved into the neighbourhood'. He was one of us, He became little and walked the dusty roads and lonely streets.

If we are brothers and sisters of Christ and in Christ, then we all share the familial relationship with Abba. As it states in Galatians 4:4-6:

'But when the set time had fully come, God sent his Son, born of a woman, born under the law, [5] to redeem those under the law, that we might receive adoption to sonship. [6] Because you are his sons, God sent the Spirit of his Son into our hearts, the Spirit who calls out, *'Abba,* Father.'

He is our brother and we are His brother in the great family of God.

What do brothers and sisters do? They stick together, whether that's an army unit that is a band of brothers, a sisterhood or members of a fraternity, they watch out for and care for each other. In Proverbs 18:24, it says that there is a friend who sticks closer than a brother, how amazing is that? The great light of the world, the only begotten sinless sacrifice is your brother and mine.

Being a part

The idea and reality of belonging is so important to us from the time we are old enough to recognize others around us. As a child, at the park I remember wanting to play with the other kids and I was so happy to be on the basketball team with my friends. As a teenager seeking for belonging, it only ramps up, being in on the latest news of who likes who and getting the invite to the party on the weekend. Not belonging or not finding a social place can be incredibly lonely, damaging and imprint upon a life for a long time to come. As adults, the need to belong does not subside. Maybe it's joining a club, hanging out at the local pub or coffee shop, seeking for a people and place of acceptance. Why was the bar from the Cheers TV show such a popular place? Everybody knew your name, you were accepted.

When I think of the privilege of belonging, the passport which I wield comes to mind. No longer can you simply hop on a plane or in the car and pass into a foreign land. That little blue book (for some of you a different colour) is the key, without it there isn't much privilege, without it, you might as well stay home. Having a driver's license, residency card or any other ID doesn't cut it. It's the passport that gives you privilege. That fact that I belong to the US, I have citizenship, allows me to pass freely back into the USA, even though I don't presently live there. I still belong and there are amazing privileges that accompany belonging.

Adoption into a family is a life-changing experience for the child being adopted, the longing parents and other family members involved. Can you see the correlation? The image of our adoption into God's great family, our lives changed forevermore. The Father is elated to have another come home and the rest of the family embracing us as one of the siblings.

Chapter 24

May - June 2014

In many respects, the end of April and the beginning of May was a blur. It involved daily contact with our agency about possible children to adopt. We were blown away by the possibilities afforded to us; at the same time realizing not everyone who enters this process gets to experience the same excitement. It was heart-breaking to have so many children in need literally flood our inbox, knowing that we could only pursue one case. To be honest, if we had a huge house and unlimited finances, we'd take as many as we could, but I suppose we have to be realistic too. During this time, I chose not to blog as we were essentially listening for God's voice as to who the child or children were for us to pursue further. Fast forward to a rainy day in middle May.

Blog Post: 15th May 2014 – We are expecting a visitor

If you can picture it, I was at the gym working out on the elliptical machine, about halfway through my warmup exercise, and then a tap on the shoulder. It took me by surprise as I had headphones in and was rockin' out to some tunes while running along. Anyway, it was an employee asking if I was Earl and, if so, that I had a phone call waiting at the front desk. Now if you have ever had this type of call you'll know it is one of two things –

1. Amazing news that simply could not wait or

2. Awful news that simply could not wait.

What kind of news was this? That is what rolled through my mind as I left the machine and quickly made my way to the front desk downstairs.

I knew that it was Rebecca and from the tone of her voice I'd know the answer as to whether this was 1. or 2. It didn't take Sherlock to figure out it was AMAZING NEWS, the kind that you do stop, thank the Lord, scream it from the mountain tops and then attempt to take it all in.

On Monday, we were sent yet another profile. We have had more than we probably expected and have been interested in a quite a few. As I told some friends, only one of the profiles will be describing our future child or children. While they all tug at our heartstrings, we can't adopt all of them, in fact, only one or two at the most. One of the profiles of a sibling pair late on Monday did pique our interest and as protocol dictates we emailed our contact at the agency to ask for more information (a Child Protection Report (CPR), which is the detailed report about the child/children) The CPRs don't always come back quickly; some we have asked for we've never seen in our inbox. This is most likely because the social worker is unavailable or that child/children is already matched to another waiting adopter.

Well this requested CPR did come back, on Tuesday it was in our possession, it came in the evening so I took advantage of having a free night (my meeting was cancelled) and we sat down to dig into another detailed profile. After finishing reading and talking about it, an hour and a half later, we thought that we'd ask to have this go to the next step.

The next step is stating that we would like to have our names put forward as a potential matching couple. At this point, it is again out of our hands. Our agency worker attempts to contact the social worker and let them know of our interest. Now, we have gone this far with two other profiles and both times it came back that the social worker did not choose to see us.

This is where yesterday's phone call comes into play, at 12:15 an email came through stating that the social worker would like to meet with us, and if it works, can that be next week? To be honest, these things do not usually move that fast, but it works for us and them, so it's on.

As you have seen with our process, it happened in quick bursts and periods of idleness. This is not easy to manage emotionally as we found it difficult to prepare ourselves for the next action. Sometimes that would be happening straight away while other times the plan wouldn't be in place for another month. This was one of those 'another month' occasions.

Blog Post: 20th May 2014 – Waiting for Takeoff

They say the best things in life are worth waiting for. If this is accurate, then we have quite a cupboard full of best things. It feels as though we have had many opportunities to wait (I totally recognize that almost everyone does and could pen a blog about their life situations), whether that be for a sign-off on paperwork, the visa application which was at a stand-still or for the right house to be available to be able to move to. So, when we found out that we'd be waiting for our meeting with visiting social workers for about a month longer than originally expected, we were both gutted and prepared at the same time.

Last week, we broke the great news that we are being visited by social workers of a sibling group. This is going to happen but it is going to be in mid-June rather than this week. We found out the news on an email whilst waiting to check out from ASDA just after we'd created a to do list for the imminent visit. Was it difficult? Yes. Did we see some real positives? Yes. Firstly, our social worker can be present at the meeting; secondly, we have more time to prepare, and thirdly, we are able to do the alternate requested date, so no diary shuffling is needed.

To be honest, having that meeting this week would have been extremely quick, maybe we are used to moving at a snail's pace, but when I looked back at my prayer journal from last Tuesday morning the siblings we are interested in weren't even in my journal. That was only a week ago, goes to show how fast aspects of this process can move.

We'll keep you all up to date with the proceedings, although there may not be much to say as we are back in a holding pattern. It feels like we are in a plane on the tarmac and have been told that we can taxi to the runway for take-off but must wait for clearance from the tower before rolling down the runway and lifting off. To take the analogy further, the engines are humming, the tray-tables are up and all baggage is safely stowed in overhead cabins. Our seat belts are on and we are simply awaiting the roar of the engine as it picks up enough ground speed to hit the air. If you've flown, you know the anticipation and excitement that hits when the plane takes that turn. There is no other plane ahead and the thrust of the machine puts you straight back in your seat. We are in that anticipating position.

It was back to 'regular' living, this time with a different decision and time frame in mind that we were wrestling with. As expected, we needed more support than normal at this point. It was not easy to keep a clear head, and without any family close by, we felt swamped emotionally.

Blog Post: 4th June 2014 – Sometimes You Can't Make it on Your Own

What is the church? That is a question that many people ask, whether they be interested in the church or are comparing what they know to what you think. Being a church leader, it is very pertinent to my life and it is a point of conversation that arises and is a subject matter in most books that I pick up. There are many clever descriptions and definitions out there and I think I should put my hat into the ring with my own.

The church is a Christ-centered group of people; they are friends; they are family and the church are the ones who are there when you can't make it on your own. I have always thought that to be true, but never more than recently. Over the course of living here [UK] and having the great opportunity to lead the church, we have developed many deep friendships, we have truly found friends and family.

During this adoption process, there have been many ups and downs and the church has been there in the ups and downs. They have been cheerleaders when that was required, they have been prayer warriors, they have been shoulders to cry on and people with whom we have shared a special celebration meal. They have been all of these aspects of support, along with daily lifting us up in prayer and gently asking how it is going. Not demanding answers, not being intrusive, rather interested, keen to know how we are doing, as much as the 'latest news'.

How does that make us feel? Immeasurably blessed. Just a few years ago, we were a couple of Americans who they decided to invite and bring across the ocean so that we could walk with them and eventually lead. A gamble? Sure. They did not know how we would cope with the cultural changes (there are many, too many to list in a simple blog entry) or how we would handle living in the centre of a village with all of the village quirks (again too much for one blog entry). I've never thought of us as risk-takers but moving here was risk and with high risk comes high reward.

The song by U2 'Sometimes You Can't Make it on Your Own' came on my iPod yesterday, while I was at the gym, and the realization of those lyrics to the title rung true in my head. I totally know that we can't make it on our own without Jesus as Saviour and the Holy Spirit leading and guiding, but I also know that we can't without others too. I have heard the term 'church-goer' used before. I don't like or use it because we are the church, the people are the church community, we don't just 'go', we are.

The saying that it takes a village to raise a child is so true; we have seen this in our experience many a time. During this adoption process, we were reminded time and again of the need for others to talk, cry and celebrate with.

Our meeting did take place. It was actually very straightforward and quite obvious to all present that we were the right dad and mom match. On the 17th June, it was one of those times of celebration.

Blog Post: 17th June 2014 – C'mon let's celebrate!

There are so many reasons to celebrate in life and in our lives specifically, but firstly we want to celebrate our Lord and Saviour Jesus who has walked with us through all the ups and downs of adoption. In the Bible, in Psalm 68:6, it says that God sets the lonely in families and, later in the Bible, it reads that we are adopted sons/daughters of the Lord - what a great family to belong to!

While we have carried some deflating news at times through this process, Monday the 16th at 11:10 the phone call was anything but deflating. We've had other phone calls like this, way back in Feb 2013 when we heard we could do a Skype interview with the American agency to our call with the agency here in the UK. There was also the elation of the approval call that we had eagerly desired for close to a month. They were exciting and encouraging, but still only a signpost on this twisting and turning road. The call on Monday morning was more than just a signpost it was more like a convergence onto a new roadway. It was to state that we have been officially linked for an adoption. You are probably interested in some details, here are some to whet the appetite...

We have been linked with two little girls, aged 1 and 3, who are from the northern part of England.

We have always been interested in adopting two and after looking at many profiles and having oodles of emails back and forth with our wonderful agency, we are so excited to be linked with these two little girls. There is much to do before the adoption takes place. We have a trip there in mid-July to meet people in their lives and another trip in late July for a matching panel meeting.

At that meeting, it is determined by a panel of professionals and adopters if we are in fact the right mom and dad for these two. Provided that the panel approves us and the decision is ratified, then after another couple of weeks we then proceed back there to be introduced to the girls, stay near the foster home and be around more and more, until eventually bringing them back to our home in the late summer.

At that point, we just let ourselves dream about what the future might look like. We didn't make any drastic changes to the house or go out and buy furniture, clothes or toys. There was no rush. It was only June at that point, plus soon we could find out what the children might like. What are their favorite colours? What kind of toys do they play with? How big are they? And not just from pictures, but we would soon find out in person. So at this time, these were questions we pondered and dreamed about.

Chapter 25

July 2014

When we reached mid-July 2014, our dreaming and wondering about the children did begin to change to thinking practically. This was going to be unlike any summer we'd ever had. We were meant to be going to go to our church camp, but once again those plans were waylaid by the adoption. It was no trouble, as we had plenty of jobs to do around the house; after all, if everything continued to go to plan there would be two little girls coming to join us...and quite soon.

Blog Post: 14th July 2014 – The Great Adventure

Strolling through our village the other day, for some reason, I was reminded of an art print we had once that was signed by famous Christian music artist Steven Curtis Chapman. It was a vividly coloured desert-like scene with a horse that had its front legs up, just raring to race towards the distant mountains. What that horse was headed for was 'The Great Adventure', as the album and picture were called. Our lives have never been labelled 'The Great Adventure' but we certainly have had some along the way. We now enter into the final stages of our adoption process, probably feeling a bit like the horse who was so ready to be released into the wild, able to gallop and run freely in the open air.

We remember fondly the day that we received the news of being officially linked with two little girls for adoption. We were in a prayer meeting with a bunch of other church leaders.

Sometimes when people pray for each other they see a picture/object that relates to the person who they are praying for at the time. This happened to us as one of the ladies who prayed for us said that she saw a hot air balloon which had been flying around, being blown here and there by the wind. That balloon was now going to come to rest on the ground and, at that point, we could exit the balloon. Once safely on the ground, we could then get on with the next part of life, which was farming. We are by no means farmers but we'd be well up for fruit in our ministry and family.

This meant so much to us, as we certainly had felt blown around by this process. To have a clear descend toward the ground sounded perfect and now to be about ready for touchdown safely on the ground. These were very encouraging words to us, they totally confirmed what we were going through at the time, and to have the phone call come just before she spoke this to us was wonderful.

This week we have the opportunity to meet a number of people who have been in the girls' lives; it is called a life appreciation day. We certainly appreciate it, a chance to ask questions, hear stories, gather information, and hopefully see some more pictures. There is a myriad of questions we have. Many are practical as we are attempting to prepare a bedroom, and set up another area of the house that will be a real child zone. What toys and clothes do they already have? What do we need to buy? We really look forward to meeting these significant people and to having some of our questions answered.

As you can imagine, we are totally stoked. This is our first trip to the local authority where the girls are presently and we'll be making another one later this month for the matching panel meeting. We also have another jaunt in August which is planned as well. The meetings, emails and phone conversations are all part of the great adventure, one that we have been so blessed to embark upon over the last few years.

During this time, we were filled with excitement most days. Sure, there were the daily tasks that needed doing but the finish/start line was coming into view. At times, it felt like our full-time job was the adoption process, as there were many emails, meetings and journeys to be taken, but we loved it all!

Blog Post: 24th July 2018 - Showers of Blessing

We turned up in the UK 6 years ago yesterday, to say we are blessed would be an understatement. It is amazing when you look around our home, you can count on your fingers the household items that we actually bought. The amount of man hours that have been accumulated in helping us move house 3 times and in helping with DIY projects is quite staggering too. We have been on the other end of generous monetary gifts as well, throughout our time, whether it has been to help with travel expenses, everyday expenses or to take a special holiday.

They say that April is a month of showers and while true, I think that July showers are quite awesome too. Allow me to explain. Last night, I went out to my friends to play Dominion, while Rebecca had a special evening, the kind that whole photo albums are dedicated toward. Some friends from our church, spearheaded by our friend Jo, put on a baby shower for her. It was held at the hall where we gather for our church meetings. How many times has she gone out the door for someone else's baby shower? I'm not sure, but it's been quite a few. It was very exhilarating seeing the excitement on her face as she came down the stairs in her beautiful dress ready to go to her baby shower!

There was a large group of women who came along to join in the festivities. I was told that they played some fun games, enjoyed food together and watched as Rebecca unravelled the gifts from paper and gift bags. Last week we were blessed to be given some practical gifts from friends in the village, then we bought a buggy, and we've been looking at beds and other practical items.

The shower gifts weren't practical. They were toys – musical, bath, cooking, dress up, a paddling pool, art easel, DVDs, CDs, books – the kind of stuff that is downright fun to open up and play with ourselves. We have had basically no toys in this house till now, but soon there will be misplaced Duplo blocks, little doll dresses, a favourite book and the like…a bit of searching for lost items sounds like fun to me.

The prep is going swimmingly as we carry on getting the bedroom and front room ready. This past week, we were blessed with a gift from the church and in the card it mentioned a 'Wendy house'. I was not familiar with the term, for those of you that aren't also, it is a playhouse, not so much a little plastic one but a proper wooden building, like a small shed. We researched a bit, with the help of Lizzie, and found a great spot in the garden and actually bought it on Monday on the spot. By Tuesday, there was already a group of guys from the church who have agreed to collect it, even the ground and build the Wendy house. We have so enjoyed the showering of the giving, care and joy of so many friends around us, yup the showers of July are a real blessing.

The showers of blessing in the month of July carried on, as you'll read we did not have a long and tenuous wait with the next matching panel.

Blog Post: 29th July 2014 – 'The Now and Not Yet' - A YES from Matching Panel

The above phrase was one that took a place in the lore of our Bible college year, as numerous visiting speakers used this phrase when talking about the Bible. I had never heard of the 'now and not yet' until 7 years ago sitting in the Vale Room in Oxford. Essentially, it is a way of looking at how the Bible explains the growth of the Kingdom of God throughout time. It is growing here on earth presently, which is the now, but also recognising that there is much which has not happened yet, it will in time but not yet. While it is a great statement for the Kingdom of God, it could take meaning for a wider variety of aspects of life too.

While driving back from our matching panel meeting this afternoon, Rebecca and I were searching for the metaphor or phrase we'd use to describe today. That familiar one 'the now and not yet' sprang to mind. There is much we are processing daily, whether that be acquiring something for the girls' bedroom, maybe it's car seats or some children's books. It feels like daily something is added to the temporary holding point of the front room, where gifts and purchases are being stashed.

Seemingly daily, there are emails or some kind of communication with our agency or with a local authority pertaining to dates and details. There are the more than daily conversations we have together. There are updates to friends who we bump into in the village or seeing people at some type of church gathering. All of this is now, it is present, it is exciting and, at times, quite exhausting. It feels like we are preparing on speed, after only figuring out what we really needed less than a fortnight ago from today.

The meeting today was also 'now'; it was another milestone on the journey that we have now passed. The matching panel gives their approval to perspective adopters after reading their information and the children's information, along with an interview-type meeting. Today, we sat in front of a group of 12 people, some on the panel and also some social workers. Unlike some interviews, we had a list of the questions which we were going to be asked, being able to work through our possible answers ahead of time was really helpful. The whole morning went exactly as planned. There were no curve balls. There was nothing which surprised or frustrated us. Much like the last time we went to panel, we felt the prayers of so many others with us in both the waiting room and the board room. We have now travelled past the matching panel and on we go into the 'not yet'.

There is no doubt that we are relishing the 'now'; it's a special time of preparing. By no means do we want to just look to the next stage or the next important meeting, but I have to admit we do. We all do! It's in the 'Not yet' where life gets very interesting. Isn't it fun to ponder what's next? Where might I be in two years, five years, what about in retirement? While it is so important to live in the present, it's also human nature to think about the 'not yet'.

The final question today was along the lines of what are our hopes for the future of the girls? It was a special question, it wasn't only about how we might handle a situation or what kind of support system we have around us. It was a query with emotion attached, it was one that brought tears to both of our eyes as we answered. A question like that really deserves an extended time to think about before attempting to formulate an answer.

It's the kind of question that you discuss when lying outdoors at night staring at the stars or gazing at the cloud formations rolling by on a summer's day. I suppose it's a recipe of blue-sky thinking mixed in with expectations, a bit of planning, a whole lot of flexibility and more than a dash of prayer. I know enough about children that there aren't blueprints drawn up as to how they will develop and grow into who they are. There are not formulas which can simply be plugged in and then your child/children will be what you planned or expected. I think that the excitement will be in watching them figure that out, seeing them be creative, trying new things, sometimes succeeding, sometimes failing, but growing into who they are through it all. That's the hope, that they will grow into who they are meant to be.

The hurdles had been jumped at this point. The matching panel was in the rear-view mirror. At this point, we were starting the purchasing process: getting beds, bedding, being given clothes by friends who knew our story and loads of toys too that were donated to us. There was always a bit of trepidation in buying and preparing before an absolute final 'yes', but we truly believed that *finally* that final 'yes' was going to be ours.

Chapter 26

You are Called Heir

All This is Yours

In 2013, a very special birth took place in England. Actually, all births are special, amazing and a gift of God. When the Duchess of Cambridge gave birth to baby George, the whole world watched with excitement as the third heir to throne was announced, another in the long line, who could one day be the king of the United Kingdom and the Commonwealth. He was a child born with more fanfare and notoriety than any other, a baby born with a title; the 'next in line'.

What comes with that moniker? Fame and wealth, along with the scrutiny of the public eye, paparazzi trains and, ultimately, power. Being in the monarchy now, compared to hundreds of years ago, probably does not capture the reality of power as it used to. The King or Queen was in charge, at their command armed forces were engaged, taxes were collected and cathedrals were built. Nowadays, it is admittedly more of a figurehead position but, nonetheless, it is still a great place of authority and responsibility. There is a vast amount of power that accompanies being the next in line or being an heir.

An heir is somebody who has the right to an inheritance. He or she has the ability to possess the land, wealth or property of the family. We're not talking about a performance-based contract, like in professional sports where somebody who plays in 150 games gets a bonus or, if he makes the All Star team, he makes an additional $75,000. This heirship, much like sonship, is not based on a contract or the performance under the agreement; it is based on position and who you are. An heir may not be the person who would likely benefit the most or he/she may not even be well respected by the public. No reason that can be found excludes them from the right of the inheritance; it's based on who they are, not what they do.

The Story of Inheritance

Jesus laid this principle out in story form in the 15th Chapter of Luke. After sharing the parables of the lost coin and lost sheep in verse 11, he upped the ante, he significantly raised the bar; he shared about a lost son. Not some object, not even a prized animal, rather flesh and blood, a son who had gone astray. A son who by anybody's standard would not have recourse to an inheritance or to a loving relationship with his father. A son who not only blew his father's money on wild living, he also had nothing to show for his life but a dreaded job of feeding pigs and scrounging out a meagre living.

As Jesus explained in this story, a picture was painted of a greedy son dwelling in squalor. He had the lowest job and position which would be a Jewish boy's worst nightmare. There was also the detesting older brother who could not fathom that this brother of his could be accepted and be part of the family. The other character that Jesus introduced was the forgiving father. So often, this parable is called the 'prodigal son', but I believe it is much more about a forgiving father, than a son who fled the scene.

When the son demanded his inheritance early, he was stating that he wished his father were dead. He was exclaiming with actions to the community around him: "if only my dad were dead, I could have my share of the money". The father gives him what he requests. He grants him an early inheritance, after all, the young man was in line to receive it. This was at a great cost to the loving father, who probably had to sell some of his property, along with losing some of his honour. To be willing to give the son his share of the inheritance at that point was an incredible sacrifice in many ways. The old saying, 'watch out what you wish for' comes true in this story as the sudden wealth proved impossible to manage.

After the expected squandering of the finance, the son found himself in the lowest of the low, not only feeding the swine, but eating their feed too. At this point, he hatched a plan to travel back home, groveling to have a position of slave in his father's house. Not a treasured son enjoying life with the family, rather one of the group who watched after the estate; one who would not have freedoms or much choice. He hoped to be a hired-hand, a worker who would come in and out of the estate at the wishes of the father. What a reversal to take place in this son's mind and heart, as he was greeted by a sprinting father.

A Loving Father

Men didn't run in that middle-eastern culture, respected leaders in a community definitely didn't run where the whole village could be watching him. Fathers also didn't run towards their sons who had all but disowned them, wished they were dead and fruitlessly spent their part of the family's fortune. The son who was aiming for a position of slaveship was accepted and given the place of sonship. Rather than walking barefoot, he was shod with sandals, the family ring was placed on his finger and his soiled clothing covered by a coat. This was the same cloak reserved for those who were special and revered, the coat which was most likely the father's.

A feast was thrown in his honour, the fatted calf prepared and the community invited to celebrate the return of the son. This was the kind of feast that would only happen in the most joyous of occasions. The level of love showed by the father, the same man who was wished dead just a few verses before, is an extreme amount of love. This was an over-the-top explanation by Jesus of an over-the-top reaction of love by the father. This is much like the response of love that each and every one of us is given as we return to the Lord as our Father. He is ready with the sandals, ring, cloak and fatted calf, a celebratory feast of life and life eternal in our honour.

Did he deserve this acceptance? Did he deserve the position of son? Those weren't the questions rolling around the father's mind. My son is home! That's what he was thinking, and how to celebrate in glorious technicolour? My son has a second chance; we have a second chance! While his status, place in society, where and how he lived had all changed, one constant remained; he was a son, an heir.

Second and Third Chances

He was afforded a seemingly unwarranted second chance. There is such power in being an heir, in being awarded the chance to carry on the family name and honour. Embedded within the structure of family is power, specifically the power to carry on to the next generation. For many children who are adopted, it is their second, third or fourth chance. They may have bounced from their original family to a foster family, to another foster family and, eventually, to an adoptive family. They may have been shuttled around to various family members who gave their all to watch after the little life but were unable to provide the care needed. Often coming from backgrounds that scream for another chance, another opportunity to be enveloped in a loving family. The lyrics of a Mumford and Sons' song rings true of the thoughts that may rumble in the mind of a young child who needs for a fresh start:

"So give me hope in the darkness that I will see the light
Cause oh that gave me such a fright
But I will hold as long as you like
Just promise me we'll be alright"

Hope is what people need especially when faced with difficult situations or decisions. It is what children need as they grow into adulthood and have to navigate through the trials of adolescence. For children who are awaiting adoption into a family, there can be such fright, an extreme unknown of how life will be lived. For those who have been placed in adoptive or fostering families, there is still much unknown and potential concern of 'how will this work for me?' Some of the same unease lies within the adults involved too. Questions of 'can we do this?' and 'are we the right ones?' pervade the mind.

Even if the child is very young and seemingly without the ability to understand, they still have attachment to who is providing care. Inside they may still ask, 'who will be there day in and day out to provide and care for me?' The question on their mind whether they can articulate it or not is, 'will I be all right?' It is not a misplaced question at all; everybody asks 'will I be all right?' in various ways and times in life. What a joy and privilege it is for adopters and foster families to offer these children more chances. More opportunities to become all they were created to be. To be able to loved and cared for, even if they have never been the recipient of that familial love before. This was the love the father showed in our story, not based on action, attitude or appearance of his son, but based on that fact he was a son.

Chapter 27

August 2014

We have now reached the final month of our long and arduous journey to adoption. Again, I don't want to make it sound like our journey is anything compared to families that face the news of a terminally ill child or stillborn baby, for example. There are so many more difficult circumstances than an adoption process.

The reality for us was that this part of the journey towards parenthood was about to come to a climax.

Blog Post: 6th August 2014 - Tomorrow is just another day you'll never forget

'Tomorrow is just another day you'll never forget' was a tagline used by Apple when introducing iTunes or some other techy gadget (actually turned out to be the Beatles available on iTunes). For us, it is a strapline we could use for the 7th of August 2014, one of those days that will quickly rise to the top of important dates in our lives. We all have them, the dates that you don't forget; the ones you don't have to look up (or least not all that often); the vital ones that carry buckets of significance.

In Biblical times, these days and events are the kinds that were remembered by either feasting or building a stone altar. Either way, they were set apart, they were celebrated and they were marked. Throughout the Holy Land, there are still little groupings of stones which stand today, built thousands of years ago. There are many examples from present day too, D-Day, the day that Kennedy was assassinated (Nov 22, 1963) or 9/11, it doesn't really need more explanation than that. There are also dates that we all remember, whether they be birthdays or wedding anniversaries, to name two that immediately spring to mind. The 3rd August 1996 in the Old Goshen Theatre is forever etched in our minds; in fact, we just celebrated our 18th by going away for an evening. There are gala times for the 20th Jan and 14th April each year. For us, there are a couple more which would probably make that list too.

The 22nd July of 2008 was one of those days, we had officially packed all our belongings in the US and headed off across the ocean to a little village in the south of England to help lead a small rural church. We did not know all that day held, but we knew that it was the beginning of a brand new chapter, if not a whole new book altogether.

Then along came the 17th Jan of 2010 when we 'took on' the leadership of West Basingstoke Community Church, what a day surrounded by friends from all over the country and the overwhelming support of the local church. At that point, we didn't know what it would feel like to plot the way forward, to have the buck stop here and to be the voice of the people. I'll never forget the feeling on the Monday morning walking down the stairs realizing what had happened the previous day, there was a new authority and responsibility that can't really be explained.

The 15th of September 2011 is another one, not as exciting or life-changing as the others but important nonetheless. That is the day that we made the phone call looking into adoption, we were able to connect with an agency in America who we eventually worked through for over two years. We also were able to speak with the embassy in this country to find out that we could use an American agency even though we were living here;

what amazing news that was.

Could we have predicted that close to three years later the culmination of many forms, meetings, trips here and there, emails, phone calls and prayer times would be taking place?

That is tomorrow, it is the pinnacle of the last three years. We set eyes on the girls tomorrow, we spend time with them tomorrow, we personally enter their lives tomorrow. Has it been a long road? You bet. Has it been excruciating at times? Absolutely. Would we have rather been another couple who saw their dreams come true without much, if any heartache? Maybe, but we have a bit of understanding of walking through pain and difficult times, the kind that many other people do as well. We look at the scores of people we have walked with, the numerous ones we've been able to encourage and the times where many have been called to pray on our behalf and we've seen faith enacted before our very eyes. So, the 7th of August 2014 is just another day, that's true, but it's one that we'll never forget.

For the next blog entries, the setting is the same. Rebecca and I were staying in a bed and breakfast, and daily going to be with the girls in their foster home. At this, point the meetings had all but ceased, this was real life for children with their foster family, in the very home where the girls had been living for a number of months.

Blog Post: 7th August 2014 - Starting Introductions

What would we feel today, what would we experience today? These were questions rolling around our minds as we went to an introduction meeting and then an hour later to meet the girls. This was a day that we've been looking forward to for nearly three years now, to say we lapped it up would be an understatement. How do you begin to explain what's it like walking into a house and there are two little girls eager to meet you? Actually, they are our daughters and we're mommy and daddy. (It does still have to go through the court hearing before being totally official)

The first words we heard today, as we eagerly opened the door, were “mommy and daddy”. I can't say that we expected that, maybe after a couple of days or a couple of hours, but not the first words that we'd hear. I've attempted to reflect on those moments and take pictures in my mind so that they are not lost, ever. They are the type of moments that Kodak calls for, or the kind that Instagram or Snapchat tend to catch, but on this occasion, it wasn't to be disrupted by the camera or mobile, it was for our eyes and ears only.

After all this time, to be seated in the foster carer’s front room, interacting with the girls, playing with one, while the other toddled around, or holding one while the other did a puzzle. It didn't matter what we did. Actually, the younger one fell asleep on my lap, that was bliss just relaxing there together.

At some point, we'll capture some pics and video, but for now we're relishing in the experience and taking mental pictures. We have literally just met them today for the first time and already see interesting traits, personality likenesses and have made memories from just an hour and half together. As I said to someone yesterday, now that we have reached this point, it is actually the beginning and that means more memories than you can count are on their way!

Blog Post: 8th August 2014 – Second Day of Introductions

Well, more memories were created today, as we walked through the door, there they both were; one with a cheeky grin and the younger one waving and saying 'hiya'. They understood who we were and that we had come to be with them, to play, interact and, simply, be. We were there for three hours, to be honest, it felt like hardly more than a half-hour, it went so quickly. There was a bit of crying here and there, lots of laughter, a bit of reading, painting and playing peekaboo. It felt normal. It was one of our concerns and prayers, that we could be at the foster carer's house and it would just be normal.

Often in life we are not looking for normal, it's either a let-down or maybe even a failure if it's just 'normal'. Many times, we think we need the optional extras, or as McDonalds made famous, not just a meal but a supersize meal. Something without the bells and whistles might be looked down on, but for us, right now, it's great to have it – a regular feeling Thursday and Friday. We'll see what the rest of the weekend has in store, probably a visit to a soft play area, along with more time at the home. Then, next week, more adventures and memories will no doubt be made.

The days of the introductions were ever so special. They are a time unlike any other and they cannot be replicated. We were smitten to be there, lapping up each moment, both with the girls and in our little cottage where we were staying, as we found space to relax and rewind.

Blog Post: 12th August 2014 - If three's company then four's a crowd

There is more than a subtle difference between going to the park and avoiding the park. It's simple, but now we go to the park. We play on the swings, ride down the slide, and generally run about. Another place that is off limits without kids are soft play areas. Instantly, they are now destinations, not reasons for a detour. What fun the soft play area was, little tikes from wall to wall, no place to plop down with our stuff, myriads of noises from toys and kids alike. After a bit, we caught our collective breaths and found a couple of spots at a table. Whether it was the ball pool, crawling gym, toddler toys or riding toys, it was all a blast.

When it was time to pause for a drink, the girls were just a bit shattered, they and we had played hard for over an hour, it was time for a break. It's weird to think that these places, like the park and soft play area, are ones that we'll seek out from now on, after many years of actively not finding out where they were.

Today, it was another kid-friendly space, the farm. There were all sorts there; pigs, cows, rabbits and a huge play area. We enjoyed it all while dodging rain drops and attempting to navigate two push chairs, some of the time carrying one, but you get the idea. To give a bit of perspective to our time at the introductions, it has been building slowly. From just a morning together, for example, up to today when we were there all day, including the bedtime routine. As you can imagine, there is much to learn and a quick learning curve, but all is well. We are figuring out how to be four.

Life is fun with 4; getting into two car seats, two buggies for a walk, two meals for them and food for us, it's all just a bit complicated. Yesterday, we were in and out of the car repeatedly here and there, then to and from appointments at the doctors and optometrist. It wasn't a day full of 'fun' stuff, but it was a day full of life.

One memory that will stick in our minds was when we got in the car and our oldest one exclaimed, "follow that SpongeBob daddy", that meant to follow the car ahead which had SpongeBob sun shades on the back windows. Now, whenever we get in the car, that's what we do! That's what this week is all about, building trust, understanding and a string of memories with each other.

As you can see, memories are a big deal to us. It's what we carry with us as people. The possessions and settings may change, the people around may change, but the memories are there. Sure, they do fade over time, and many will be lost forever, but some stick. I suppose the more you make, the likelihood of remembering some of them gets higher, that's what we're shooting for.

Blog Post: 16th August 2014 - Home again for the first time

Fri. am - Home is where we dwell, it's a place of comfort, it's a place of known. How often do you walk into a building attempting to grasp where is a toilet or what floor is the office on? In a shopping mall or amusement park, it might even take a map to figure it all out, where the exits are and the shops you are most interested in finding.

At home, that's not true. It's known. You don't have to familiarize yourself with the surroundings. Today, we drive back home, except on this occasion it will be different. There will be a room that is a new colour, it will have newly hung blinds, pics on the wall and two little beds ready for two little girls.

For us, going back home is a welcome occasion. We've had an amazing time during the introductions, getting to see and understand routines, taking trips to appointments, to the shops, and out for fun to the park and even an aquarium. For Rebecca and me, the drive home will be a time to reflect upon this week and certainly to look forward to the coming days, months and years. It dawned on me again yesterday while driving that we weren't babysitting for friends of ours, sure that's fun to do, but this is so totally different.

Fri. pm – A raft of excitement hit us as we got closer to home, that final stretch seemed longer than normal somehow. Not only were we glad to get back to see Lizzie and Nooma, and to unpack, we were also going to see the girls' bedroom. We had great reason to believe that it would be amazing, with our friends' (Lizzie, Louise and Carol) talents all on display. There is decal of I Samuel 1:27 above the door it reads:

I Samuel 1:27 – For this child I have prayed and the Lord has granted the desires of my heart

Walking in the room was an experience to remember, with the multi-coloured painted hot air balloons and fluffy white clouds on the wall, along with bespoke fairy lights and bedding. It's a real dream-room for the girls to call their own and begin life here with us.

Saturday am. - Today has been all about last minute preparation. Whether it is putting a couple things in the loft, finding a home for this toy or that stuffed animal, putting up stair gates and safety locks on drawers. The home has been a hive of activity, all for two little lovely ladies. They too are excited to be coming 'home' (even if they don't know it as home yet).

Imagine if you were going to a new home, one that was not known. Try to think if it was your third home this year, how worried and concerned you might be. This will be their third home, they will not be bringing much with them, they don't have much to bring. For children in care, they often are coming from difficult home situations where it doesn't feel like home, home is not where the heart is. In fact, it is usually quite the opposite, it is a place of struggle, with bad or scary memories and associations. Home may not be seen as a place of comfort, fun and security, now imagine if you were coming into another new home.

Saturday pm. – Today, they came home for the first time (cue tears), seeing their smiling faces when they recognized a toy or book that was sent with them was priceless. Hearing the excitement when they found a new toy or book which is now theirs was even more exciting. When we all trailed upstairs to their room to see them lay eyes on their bed, soft toys and decorated walls was unforgettable. They don't sleep here for a couple more nights, but soon a new home will be a new normal. Can't wait to see what the next couple of days have in store for us all. There will be no doubt much more 'new', whether that be the garden, park, nap time or bath time. Are we all blessed or what!?

At this point the introductions were over. We were home, simply back home, except this time with two in our charges. Our home would never be the same, and we didn't want it to be, the sounds of crying and laughter filled the halls and rooms.

Blog Post: 19th August 2014 - The 'handover' is complete!

Completeness is an accomplishment, we've all done it. You've no doubt had a daunting project, a looming deadline or a seemingly unclimbable mountain to ascend. That's a bit of what the adoption journey has felt like, with the last couple of weeks being the penultimate push to the summit. There is one more action to take to reach the pinnacle (a court celebration where they become 'Robinsons', legally) but that is down the road in a few months. For now, we'll enjoy this view. This evening it is one from our home, while Rebecca and I sit downstairs on our computers and for the first time in our house, our girls sleep peacefully upstairs.

That is weird to say as we've never said it before, never before have we been downstairs while precious ones sleep upstairs. The introductions have gone well and the last step of the introductions is the handover. This is essentially when the foster carers say goodbye at their apartment in town and we all bundle in the car and drive home for good. That all happened this morning, today was not easy as you can imagine.

There is much emotion tied up with everyone involved. There has been some crying, whimpering and general frustration. Is this unexpected? Not at all. This is not just a slight change, this is a life change, change for good and for the good. The girls have had an amazing experience at their carers' house and we have learned many valuable lessons from them over the last couple of weeks. It's now up to us, whether that be day-to-day actions like feeding, changing, bathing or long-term things like healthcare and going to school.

Blog Post: 20th August 2014 - Folgers coffee used to have the tagline 'the best part of waking up is Folgers in your cup'

I don't agree with that. As much as I might enjoy a cup of joe, the best of waking up today was not coffee in my cup but two little ones coming into our room. The youngest one, who was crying when she awoke, was brought in by Rebecca and then a minute later the older crawled into our bed as well.

What a way to wake up! This after a great night of rest, that's right they both slept all night in their new beds and new home on the first night ever sleeping here. I know I've said it before but it's the little things that are the most entertaining, whether it be sharing breakfast together, reading books or seeing the excitement on their little faces when we do something fun.

Because so much of what we have around here is new to them, it is great finding creative activities and unread books which quickly become favourites in our library. We already have two book baskets going (we're both ex elementary teachers what can we say). Today was also our first trip out, all the way to the park, which is about a one-minute walk as the crow flies, just up the road from our house. We've wondered, what will the new normal look and feel like? We're not sure and believe me, we aren't there yet, and probably won't be for quite some time. There is way too much that is new and exciting to find a definite pattern to each day, every one full of unique adventures and discoveries.

Chapter 28

The Beginning

Often in life the end and the beginning can be simultaneous for each other, such is our narrative. As one journey ends, the next begins, and so carries on the story.

The years preceding August 2014 were about waiting, preparing, praying, taking action and, simply, living our lives.

For us, the ending is so much sweeter than we could have ever dreamed, imagined or created in our own strength. What we once thought would be our cosy little family of three, is actually four. The new beginning has started, we have been blessed with two little girls. I could pen another whole book about parenthood or do a blog about family life as a dad of two, but the journey of this book is complete...I think I hear Amy or Katrina calling me to come and play.

Chapter 29

An Unexpected Chapter

As it has happened so many times in our lives, we get phone calls during prayer gatherings. The morning of the 11th January 2016 was one of those calls. It was Rebecca. Like previous calls, I could tell something huge was up. We had been contacted, well in advance, to be told that our girls were going to be older sisters. The council had contacted our adoption agency to ask if we might be interested in having another child.

We were taken aback. It's not the kind of request you expect on a wintry January morning, especially after we had really settled in to being 'us'. Over the next couple of weeks, we did some soul searching, talked to our trusted friends and mothers, to arrive at a 'yes'. We felt it was the right thing to enter the adoption process once again.

You'll be pleased to know that we did not have to do the whole process again, but we did once again enter a shortened set of homestudy meetings. These were much easier than previous but they did remind us that we were in this for the long haul. It also meant, at some point, another panel meeting. This time we trusted it would go off without a hitch.

We had essentially finished all the meetings when we were told that due to the way the council processed the adoptions, we had to have our process paused. This was not easy. At that point, we didn't know if a baby had even been born.

The pause button was pushed for about four months and then, in October, it was 'go time' again. All was cleared for us to have final meetings and to go to another set of introductions. This was a whole new experience, doing introductions with a baby, as well as with our own two girls. To say they were excited would be a bit of an understatement. Try as we did to temper their glee, it was not easy and, let's be honest, it wasn't really needed either. They were big sisters, that *is* something to be happy about.

It was a brief introduction time and before we knew it, on 30th November 2016, a six-month old was being driven to our house, where she (that's right, another girl!) would find a forever home. The main question we've asked ourselves with this adoption is, 'do we have room for her?' In our house, sort of, in our hearts...absolutely.

There has been a steep learning curve parenting a baby, but we're up for the challenge. How could we pass up a little gal who is all cheeks and teeth?! In the Psalms, there is a verse that talks about 'blessed is the man whose quiver is full of children'; ours has three, that's probably not stuffed full, but not empty either.

Once again, I need to go, I think I heard Amy and Katrina tell me that Rose was trying to get into something in the kitchen again!

ABOUT THE AUTHOR

I am a passionate follower of Jesus who is blessed to be a husband to Rebecca, father of three girls, pastor of the Community Church and a friend to many. I have been married for over 20 years and have lived in the UK since 2008 and, previously, in Indiana, USA, after growing up in upstate New York. I love to spend time with my family, play board games, watch American sports, and, if space, to play guitar and sing.

Reason for Writing

I have not written a book before but I did blog all throughout our adoption process, as a way to keep our friends and family informed. This turned out to be widely read with hundreds of page views routinely with over 21,000 visits, while I was doing the blog. I was encouraged by the well-known author, Mark Buchanan, that 'I have a book in me'. I knew that this book had to be our adoption story, which could be interspersed with the story of family in the Bible., which is also so important to me.

Did you enjoy the book?

Thank you for joining me in retelling the journey of our family and perspectives on the great family of God. I hope the stories touched your soul the way they touched mine.

Now that you have read the book if you have a minute to spare, I would really appreciate a short review on the page or site where you bought the book. Your help in spreading the word is greatly appreciated. Reviews from readers like you make a huge difference to helping new readers find stories like 'our road to adoption – the story of our family and the great family of God'.

Thank you!

earl d robinson

Made in the USA
Middletown, DE
13 May 2022

65719793R00139